JOSHUA ZERMENO

DISOBEYING AN UNLAWFUL ORDER

A SPACE FORCE OFFICER'S FIGHT FOR FREEDOM

For those who stood their ground—and paid the price.

"One has not only a legal but a moral responsibility to obey just laws. Conversely, one has a moral responsibility to disobey unjust laws."

- Martin Luther King Jr.

Contents

Abbreviations and Acronyms

ADC – Area Defense Counsel: A military legal service providing defense representation to service members facing disciplinary actions.

ASAP – As Soon As Possible: A term indicating urgency, often used in military orders.

BCMR – Board for Correction of Military Records: A military board responsible for correcting military records.

BMT – Basic Military Training: The initial training program for Air Force enlisted recruits.

COVID / COVID-19 – Coronavirus Disease 2019: The virus and pandemic that prompted the vaccine mandate.

DoD – Department of Defense: The U.S. government department overseeing the military.

FDA – Food and Drug Administration: The U.S. agency responsible for approving vaccines.

FSF – Family Stabilization Fund: A proposed fund to support families affected by the mandate.

LAR – Leadership Accountability Review: A proposed review to investigate commanders' actions during the mandate.

LOR – Letter of Reprimand: A formal military punishment documenting failure to obey an order.

MMPD – Medical Mandate Policy Directive: A proposed policy to reform medical mandates.

MRB – Mandate Restitution Board: A proposed board to process restitution claims for affected service members.

NASA – National Aeronautics and Space Administration: The U.S. space agency involved in space missions.

NICU – Neonatal Intensive Care Unit: A specialized hospital unit providing intensive care for premature or critically ill newborns, such as the author's daughter after her premature birth.

OPR – Officer Performance Report: A formal evaluation document assessing an officer's performance, impacting promotions and career progression.

OTS – Officer Training School: A program for training Air Force officers.

POTUS – President of the United States: The President, referenced in space access initiatives.

PTSD – Post-Traumatic Stress Disorder: A mental health condition affecting individuals after trauma.

ROTC – Reserve Officers' Training Corps: A college-based program for training officers.

SECDEF – Secretary of Defense: The head of the Department of Defense.

SERE – Survival, Evasion, Resistance, and Escape: A military training program for survival skills.

SLD 30 – 30th Space Launch Delta: The unit at Vandenberg overseeing space launch operations.

SLS – Space Launch Squadron: The 2d Space Launch Squadron, the author's unit at Vandenberg.

SMC – Space and Missile Systems Center: A former Air Force organization for space launch certifications.

SpaceX – Space Exploration Technologies Corporation: A private aerospace company founded by Elon Musk, focused on space launch services and spacecraft development, known for the Falcon 9 rocket and Starlink satellite deployments.

SSC – Space Systems Command: A U.S. Space Force organization responsible for developing, acquiring, and sustaining space systems, succeeding the Space and Missile Systems Center (SMC).

UCMJ – Uniform Code of Military Justice: The legal framework governing military conduct.

UIF – Unfavorable Information File: A personnel file where reprimands are documented.

UPT – Undergraduate Pilot Training: The Air Force program for training pilots.

USD P&R – Under Secretary of Defense for Personnel and Readiness: A DoD position overseeing personnel policy.

USSF – United States Space Force: The military branch established in 2019.

VA – Department of Veterans Affairs: The agency providing benefits and care to veterans.

VASRD – VA Schedule for Rating Disabilities: The VA system for determining disability ratings.

VISP – Vaccine Injury Support Program: A proposed program for medical care for vaccine injuries.

Timeline of Key Events

2010: Enlisted in the U.S. Air Force with a degree in Mechanical Engineering Technology and a private pilot's license, beginning career as a B-52 bomber mechanic.

2013: Commissioned as an officer in the U.S. Air Force and selected for Undergraduate Pilot Training.

2015: Graduated from Undergraduate Pilot Training and earned an Air Force Pilot Rating.

2018: Transitioned to space launch operations at Vandenberg Air Force Base as a mission integrator with the 1st Air and Space Test Squadron.

March 2020: The COVID-19 pandemic began, prompting global lockdowns and military operational changes.

February 5, 2021: Commissioned as one of the first officers in the newly formed U.S. Space Force, tasked with standing up operations at Vandenberg.

August 24, 2021: Secretary of Defense Lloyd Austin issues the COVID-19 vaccine mandate for all DoD service members.

September 22, 2021: Received first Letter of Reprimand for refusing the COVID-19 vaccine.

September 29, 2021: Received a "Do Not Promote" recommendation for refusing the COVID-19 vaccine.

October 25, 2021: Received second Letter of Reprimand for refusing the COVID-19 vaccine.

October 2021: Submitted voluntary separation request in accordance with Department of the Air Force guidance, in lieu of complying with the vaccine mandate.

November 2, 2021: Banned from government buildings at Vandenberg, beginning 20 months of isolation.

February 3, 2022: Voluntary separation request officially denied.

February 9, 2022: SLD 30 Commander initiated UCMJ punishment recommendation for continued refusal to comply with the vaccine mandate.

June 2022: UCMJ punishment initiated by SSC commander for ongoing non-compliance.

September 2022: UCMJ punishment continues with additional coordination.

January 10, 2023: COVID-19 vaccine mandate rescinded by the Department of Defense; Secretary of Defense orders correction of all records and removal of adverse actions.

January 2023: Discharge board proceedings and UCMJ punishment dropped following mandate rescission.

February 2023: Notified of second failure to promote and informed of involuntary separation.

August 31, 2023: Involuntarily separated from the Space Force after 13 years of service due to vaccine refusal.

January 27, 2025: President Trump signs an executive order to reinstate service members discharged for refusing the vaccine, with back pay.

April 23, 2025: Secretary of Defense Pete Hegseth declares the vaccine mandate unlawful, validating the author's stand.

Prologue

Some mornings I wake before the sun, my body still wired to the rhythm of a life I no longer live. In the early quiet, the house holds the soft rustle of four children beginning to stir—backpacks slung over shoulders, cereal bowls clinking, and shoes lined up by the door. My life revolves around them now. I'm a father before all else: making lunches, checking homework, driving to school, coaching youth sports, and being the steady hand when emotions run high.

At night, after dinner is cleaned up, the day's activities are complete, and teeth are brushed, I tuck each of the kids into bed. Then I lie down in my own room, alone, and listen to the silence—not the peaceful kind, but the kind that lingers after something has been broken. My wife and I live in separate homes now. I raise my three children in mine, she raises her two in hers, and together, we raise our youngest, Constance. Born at just 1 pound, 8 ounces, she is the very definition of a miracle. Even with all we've lost, we continue trying to rebuild what was taken.

We live just miles from Vandenberg Space Force Base and the SpaceX launch site where I used to work. When rockets go up, the ground trembles, and neighbors gather outside to watch. My kids and I rush to the porch, eyes lifted. I stand behind them, sometimes with neighbors, sometimes on my own, and feel each launch shake something loose inside me. I spent years working those missions—planning them, managing teams of engineers and Space Force personnel, solving problems no manual could predict. It wasn't just about launching a rocket—it was about shaping the future of space exploration and pushing humanity further into the stars. That work mattered. I believed in it.

Now, those launches remind me of what could have been. I should still be part of it—still wearing the uniform, still briefing missions, still leading.

Instead, I'm left with going-away gifts signed by teammates and awards from every assignment I touched in thirteen years. No photos in uniform. No framed medals on the wall. Just quiet reminders of a career that ended in silence.

This memoir isn't written out of bitterness. It's written because I chose to stand for something. When an order came down that I knew in my gut was wrong—legally murky, morally dishonest, and personally unjust—I didn't bend. And when the cost came, I bore it. My children are watching. Every day, they're watching. One day, they'll ask why I made the choices I did.

This is the story I'll tell them.

Introduction

For 13 years, I had the privilege of working countless maintenance, air, and space operations alongside thousands of amazing individuals in the Air Force and Space Force, believing the military stood for unyielding freedom. Those years were defined by camaraderie and purpose—wrenching on B-52 bombers as a young mechanic, serving on aircrew missions as a pilot, and later leading space launch operations at Vandenberg Space Force Base, where my team played a pivotal role in advancing our nation's space capabilities through numerous critical missions. I poured my heart into every mission, trusting that the military's foundation was built on honor, justice, and the defense of liberty. In 2021, the COVID-19 vaccine mandate shattered that illusion; it was a policy I saw as a direct assault on the values I'd sworn to uphold, a betrayal that shook the very core of my service. In the military, orders are the bedrock of service—commands that forge discipline, drive missions, and safeguard lives. Lawful orders, rooted in military law and ethical purpose, advance the greater good. Unlawful orders, however, cross a moral line, demanding actions that betray justice and honor. Distinguishing the two is a service member's burden, clouded by hierarchy, the weight of tradition, and the ever-present threat of consequences. I disobeyed an order to receive the vaccine, believing it unlawful, a decision that came at a profound personal cost—I knew my family would bear the brunt alongside me, and the system I trusted struck back with a vengeance.

For two years, I endured psychological warfare—relentless persecution, isolation, and career sabotage—that tore my family apart, obliterated my 13-year career, and left damage that can never be undone. I hid my struggle from my children to protect them, shielding them from the harsh reality of their father being branded an outcast, banned from base, and stripped of purpose, all while grappling with the weight of my decision. This memoir is my raw, unfiltered reckoning: an exposé that dismantles the military's false narratives, revealing a mandate that crushed free thinkers who dared to question right from wrong. Its brutal side effect was a purge of some of the military's sharpest minds, leaving shattered lives across every branch through coercion, public shaming, and ruthless career destruction. I was one of tens of thousands of individuals purged from service—skilled professionals whose training, experience, and institutional knowledge can't be replaced by new recruits, a loss that weakened our military's readiness at a time when global threats demand strength. The mandate didn't just break careers; it fractured families, eroded trust, and exposed a system that valued compliance over conscience.

If you're a service member, family member, or civilian who faced the mandate's iron grip and held fast to principle, this story is yours. Raw, defiant, and unflinching, these pages carry the weight of our betrayal and the fire of our resolve. This is where the truth breaks free, and the fight for honor lives on—a battle cry for accountability, for those who stood their ground, and for the restitution we deserve after enduring a betrayal that shook the very foundation of our service.

Education | Awards | Achievements

As I previously stated, I spent 13 years working numerous maintenance, air, and space operations with thousands of committed Air Force and Space Force members, an honor I deeply value. I enlisted in 2010 with a Bachelor of Science in Mechanical Engineering Technology and a private pilot's license, ready to serve. I attended B-52 technical training at Sheppard Air Force Base, earning top graduate honors, then was assigned to work at Barksdale Air Force Base. There, I maintained B-52 bombers, earned the Group Commander's Achievement Award for my 5-level Career Development Courses, and was certified for the Personal Reliability Program. As an Airman First Class, I pushed for more, securing spots in Officer Training School (OTS) and Undergraduate Pilot Training (UPT). Graduating second out of 17 in advanced UPT opened the door to fly the RC-135 Rivet Joint.

At Offutt Air Force Base, I tackled the demands of RC-135 operations. As Squadron Duty Officer and Wing Scheduling Executor, I coordinated operations with maintenance and flying squadrons, overseeing air refueling and contingency plans for adverse weather. My efforts helped drive 495 sorties and over 2,000 flight hours, keeping missions on track through relentless teamwork.

In 2018, my first assignment at Vandenberg Air Force Base with the 1st Air and Space Test Squadron was as a mission integrator for small spacelift operations. I later rose to Flight Commander and Assistant Director of Operations. From March 2020 to July 2021, I led an 81-member, multi-agency team to develop a remote operations plan during the COVID-19 pandemic, keeping Vandenberg's launches on track. My team of 37 executed nine flawless campaigns, successfully sending 304 satellites and two astronauts into orbit. I contributed to NASA's Ascent Abort-2 mission, oversaw Minotaur vehicle transport across four U.S. sites, managed X-37B Orbital Test Vehicle integration, maintained seven key launch facilities, and drove Western Range strategies to ensure national space access. Helping transition Vandenberg to Space Force operations was a career highlight.

Years of training shaped my path: honor graduate at Basic Military Training, top graduate at B-52 maintenance technical training, Career Development Courses, Airman Leadership Course, Crash Damaged and Disabled Aircraft Recovery Training, OTS, UPT, Survival, Evasion, Resistance, and Escape training (SERE), acquisition courses, and Squadron Officer School. This isn't about self-praise; it's to highlight the extensive training and experience purged from the U.S. military due to the COVID-19 mandate. I was one of tens of thousands of individuals removed from service.

A Question That Changed Everything

In 2001, I was a kid sitting on the couch, lacing up my shoes for school, when the news flashed images of a plane crashing into the Twin Towers. I watched, transfixed, as the footage replayed, unaware of the profound significance of that moment. I didn't know then that it would become a memory etched into my mind for life. Fast forward to January 2020, and I found myself in a strikingly similar moment of unsuspecting gravity. I was in my office when one of my lieutenants knocked and asked for a moment to talk. He settled into a chair and mentioned a "virus" he'd been hearing about on the news, asking if we had a plan in case of an outbreak on base. At the time, I hadn't heard of this virus, so I kept the conversation short and promised to keep him informed if I heard anything from higher command. Once again, I didn't grasp the weight of that conversation—a fleeting question that would spark a chain of events, forever altering the course of my life.

The Call to Return

In March 2020, I was on a rare vacation with my children and extended relatives at Universal Studios in Southern California. For a military family often separated by duty, these moments of togetherness were a lifeline— watching my children's faces light up with wonder as we explored the park felt like a stolen slice of normalcy. But when my phone rang and my commander's name flashed across the screen, a cold dread washed over me, cutting through the warmth of the day. I knew instantly that something was wrong. Stepping away from my family, I found a quiet spot near a towering ride and answered the call with a sinking heart. My commander's voice was clipped and urgent: a real-world recall was in effect. "Where are you?" he asked, his tone leaving no room for delay. I told him I was at Universal Studios with my family, my voice heavy with the weight of what I knew was coming. "Wrap it up and return to base ASAP," he ordered. I managed a single, strained word: "COVID?" "Yes," he confirmed. "Get back before lockdowns start." The words hit like a punch, and I stood frozen for a moment, the sounds of laughter and music fading into a hollow echo. With a heavy heart, I returned to my family, their joy dissolving as I explained we had to leave immediately. We shared hurried, emotional hugs with my relatives, the weight of uncertainty pressing down on us. None of us knew those rushed goodbyes would be our last in-person moments for an achingly long time, as the shadow of a global pandemic loomed ever closer, threatening to upend our lives in ways we couldn't yet fathom.

People First

When lockdowns were officially ordered in March 2020, my commander convened a meeting for squadron leadership. As one of five Flight Commanders, I attended, ready to navigate the uncertainty ahead. The meeting's top priority? Our people. The commander outlined the challenges looming in the coming days and directed each of us to develop a comprehensive plan for our respective flights. These plans had to address critical needs: ensuring everyone stayed home, supporting their families, maintaining communication, conducting daily check-ins, preparing for emergencies, guiding those who felt sick or suspected COVID, and boosting morale in the face of isolation. Once we crafted these plans, the commander reviewed and approved them. He then sent a mass email to the squadron, clearly outlining what lay ahead. Despite fears surrounding the virus, his actions set a powerful precedent: our people were the priority, and we would care for them no matter what challenges arose. This commitment shaped the squadron's culture, inspiring every member to go the extra mile to ensure mission continuity.

Mission Continuity

With our people's well-being prioritized, our commander shifted focus to mission continuity. Our squadron at Vandenberg Air Force Base (now known as Vandenberg Space Force Base) oversaw all space launch operations, a critical responsibility with no room for disruption, even during a global pandemic. The immediate challenge was determining whether rocket launches could continue safely. To answer this, our commander leveraged the expertise of the very people he had just prioritized, directing each Flight Commander to collaborate with their teams to assess what was feasible. As the Flight Commander for Bravo Flight, I led a team of engineers and technical experts responsible for fleet surveillance and mission assurance of SpaceX's Falcon 9 rocket launches at Vandenberg. In simpler terms, my flight's mission was to safeguard critical government assets during these launches, protecting military payloads on the rocket and infrastructure on the base, while balancing SpaceX's innovative approaches with strategic priorities. From the moment a booster and payload arrived at Vandenberg to the instant of launch—and landing—our team maintained oversight. We had personnel at the Space Launch Complex monitoring every step, a team in the mission control room tracking systems and updating base leadership on launch day, members coordinating with Public Affairs, and we also had team members assist SpaceX operations at Cape Canaveral Air Force Station (now known as Cape Canaveral Space Force Station).

SpaceX's advanced yet streamlined automation gave us an edge. To address the question of launching rockets during a pandemic, I tasked my engineers and experts to work closely with SpaceX to develop a remote launch capability, enabling our team to communicate, stay connected, and monitor all Falcon 9 systems remotely on launch day. Within a month, we built and tested a system, successfully demonstrating a simulated remote launch to our commander. The simulation was a resounding success, earning approval to implement remote launch operations for real-world missions. Over the course of the COVID-19 crisis, my team's remote operations supported seven SpaceX launches, delivering 304 satellites and two astronauts to orbit. As pandemic guidance evolved—masks, six-foot distancing, quarantine protocols, and testing—we gradually adjusted, allowing personnel who felt safe to return to the launch pad or mission control room while permitting others to continue using remote operations.

My Officer Performance Report for this period, endorsed by my Squadron Commander, Group Commander, and Wing Commander, credited me with developing remote-on-console operations, training an 81-member multi-agency crew, executing seven launches during the crisis, analyzing and resolving 28 risks, and putting 304 satellites and two astronauts into orbit. It recognized my management of SpaceX and NASA processing for a $37M asset, revamping the launch engineering training program, spearheading launch facility renovation to support future SpaceX launches, and reviewing 23 packages while closing 5,000 issues for National Security Space Launch new entrant certifications. The report ranked me #3 out of 26 Company Grade Officers, #3 out of 12 Flight Commanders, and noted my vital role in the 30th Operations Group's mission continuity during the COVID-19 pandemic. It recommended me for promotion to Assistant Director of Operations, Special Operations, and Professional Development Education.

This chapter isn't about my personal accolades—it's about what my team achieved while unvaccinated over 17 months in the heart of the pandemic. Our successes demonstrated that being unvaccinated was no barrier to mission success.

A New Frontier

On February 5, 2021, at the height of the pandemic and before the COVID-19 vaccine mandates would cast a shadow over my career, I received news that would mark one of the proudest moments of my life: I was selected to commission into the newly formed United States Space Force. As one of the first officers to join this fledgling branch, I felt a surge of honor and responsibility, a recognition of my leadership and expertise after 11 years of service. This wasn't just a promotion—it was a call to stand at the forefront of history, tasked with helping stand up Space Force operations at Vandenberg Space Force Base, guiding the base's transition to its new mission, and solidifying its role in national security space launches. I was stepping into a new frontier, one filled with promise, uncertainty, and the weight of building something entirely new.

The moment I received the call from my commanding officer, I was flooded with a mix of emotions. Pride swelled in my chest—I had been chosen to help shape the future of military space operations, a mission that felt both thrilling and daunting. The Space Force, established just over a year earlier in December 2019, was still in its infancy, a bold experiment to secure America's interests in the contested domain of space. Being one of the first officers to join meant I was part of a pioneering group, entrusted with turning a vision into reality. But beneath the pride, there was a quiet undercurrent of uncertainty. The world was still grappling with the pandemic—masks, social distancing, and remote work had become the norm, and Vandenberg, like every other base, was navigating uncharted waters. How do you build a new branch of the military under such conditions? How do you establish trust, cohesion, and mission readiness when the world feels so fractured?

The honor came with immense responsibility. My role at Vandenberg was to help stand up Space Force operations, a task that felt both exhilarating and overwhelming. Vandenberg had long been a hub for space launches, but transitioning to the Space Force meant redefining its mission, aligning it with the new branch's priorities, and ensuring its critical role in national security space launches. I was tasked with overseeing the integration of personnel, equipment, and protocols, ensuring that every piece fit into the larger puzzle of the Space Force's vision. This meant long hours coordinating with other officers, many of whom were also new to the branch, as we worked to establish operational frameworks from scratch. We had to rewrite manuals, develop training programs, and build a culture that reflected the Space Force's unique identity—all while adapting to the constraints of a pandemic that limited face-to-face collaboration.

Being one of the first officers also meant being a trailblazer in a very public way. The Space Force was under scrutiny—some saw it as a necessary evolution, others as an unnecessary expense. Every decision we made at Vandenberg felt like it carried the weight of proving the branch's worth. I remember standing in the mission control room, watching a Falcon 9 rocket roar into the sky, unleashing its latest high-tech payload in a blaze of futuristic glory, the ground and walls shaking around us, while American citizens across the West Coast witnessed another "UFO" sighting in the sky, a fiery streak that painted the heavens with an otherworldly glow, captivating onlookers in a cosmic spectacle. That launch, one of the first under the Space Force's banner at Vandenberg, felt like a tangible symbol of what we were building—a new era of military space operations. But behind that moment of triumph were countless sleepless nights, endless meetings over Zoom, and the constant pressure to get it right. We were entrusted with a mission that couldn't fail, not when national security depended on it.

The pandemic added another layer of complexity. In early 2021, the vaccine was still months away for most, and the military was under strain, balancing health protocols with operational demands. At Vandenberg, we faced the same challenges—limited personnel on-site, supply chain disruptions, and the ever-present fear of an outbreak derailing our progress. Yet, there was a strange sense of unity in those early days. My fellow officers and I shared a common purpose, a determination to make the Space Force a success despite the odds. We were building something bigger than ourselves, a legacy that would outlast the chaos of the moment.

Looking back, that commission on February 5, 2021, was a defining moment—a beacon of hope before the storm of the vaccine mandates would test everything I stood for. I had no idea then that the same institution I was helping to build would soon turn against me, labeling me a criminal for my moral stand. But in that moment, I felt the weight of history on my shoulders, the privilege of being part of something new, and the resolve to make it work. The Space Force was my frontier, and I was ready to chart its course—no matter what lay ahead.

Mandate Unleashed

On August 24, 2021, roughly 17 months into the COVID-19 pandemic, the Secretary of Defense issued a mandate requiring all Active Duty and Ready Reserve members of the Armed Forces, including the National Guard, under Department of Defense authority to receive the COVID-19 vaccine. Below is the full text of Secretary Lloyd Austin's memo, issued that day, which set this policy in motion:

"MEMORANDUM FOR SENIOR PENTAGON LEADERSHIP COMMANDERS OF THE COMBATANT COMMANDS DEFENSE AGENCY AND DOD FIELD ACTIVITY DIRECTORS

SUBJECT: Mandatory Coronavirus Disease 2019 Vaccination of Department of Defense Service Members

To defend this Nation, we need a healthy and ready force. After careful consultation with medical experts and military leadership, and with the support of the President, I have determined that mandatory vaccination against coronavirus disease 2019 (COVID-19) is necessary to protect the Force and defend the American people.

Mandatory vaccinations are familiar to all of our Service members, and mission-critical inoculation is almost as old as the U.S. military itself. Our administration of safe, effective COVID-19 vaccines has produced admirable results to date, and I know the Department of Defense will come together to finish the job, with urgency, professionalism, and compassion.

I therefore direct the Secretaries of the Military Departments to immediately begin full vaccination of all members of the Armed Forces under DoD authority on active duty or in the Ready Reserve, including the National Guard, who are not fully vaccinated against COVID-19. Service members are considered fully vaccinated two weeks after completing the second dose of a two-dose COVID-19 vaccine or two weeks after receiving a single dose of a one-dose vaccine. Those with previous COVID-19 infection are not considered fully vaccinated.

Mandatory vaccination against COVID-19 will only use COVID-19 vaccines that receive full licensure from the Food and Drug Administration (FDA), in accordance with FDA-approved labeling and guidance. Service members voluntarily immunized with a COVID-19 vaccine under FDA Emergency Use Authorization or World Health Organization Emergency Use Listing in accordance with applicable dose requirements prior to, or after, the establishment of this policy are considered fully vaccinated. Service members who are actively participating in COVID-19 clinical trials are exempted from mandatory vaccination against COVID-19 until the trial is complete in order to avoid invalidating such clinical trial results.

Mandatory vaccination requirements will be implemented consistent with DoD Instruction 6205.02, "DoD Immunization Program," July 23, 2019. The Military Departments should use existing policies and procedures to manage mandatory vaccination of Service members to the extent practicable. Mandatory vaccination of Service members will be subject to any identified contraindications and any administrative or other exemptions established in Military Department policy. The Military Departments may promulgate appropriate guidance to carry out the requirements set out above. The Under Secretary of Defense for Personnel and Readiness may provide additional guidance to implement and comply with FDA requirements or Centers for Disease Control and Prevention recommendations.

The Secretaries of the Military Departments should impose ambitious time-lines for implementation. Military Departments will report regularly on vaccination completion using established systems for other mandatory vaccine reporting.

Our vaccination of the Force will save lives. Thank you for your focus on this critical mission.

Signed,

Secretary of Defense Lloyd Austin"

The announcement triggered an immediate wave of questions and concerns from military members and DoD civilian employees across all levels of the chain of command. "Why is this suddenly mandatory?" "Can I opt out?" "Are exemptions available?" "Someone got vaccinated last month and still caught COVID." "Is this legal?" "Have long-term studies been done?" Every imaginable question surfaced, reflecting unease and uncertainty. Shortly after the mandate, additional guidance clarified that service members could apply for religious or medical exemptions. An email from senior leadership followed, outlining the stark options: get vaccinated or secure an approved medical or religious waiver. Those were the choices laid before us.

Vaccine Refusal

When the Secretary of Defense's vaccine mandate was issued on August 24, 2021, an uneasy feeling washed over me, unlike anything I had ever experienced. For 17 months, I had led Bravo Flight at Vandenberg Space Force Base, successfully developing remote launch operations for the Air Force and Space Force during the COVID-19 pandemic. Those operations ran flawlessly, delivering 304 satellites and two astronauts to orbit. My team had relied on common-sense precautions against a virus that, over time, proved less deadly than initially feared. I had never contracted COVID-19 myself. Yet, the mandate to vaccinate some of the fittest, most capable people in the military— people who had thrived without it—felt wrong. My gut screamed there was an ulterior motive. Nothing about the mandate sat right with me. The military's response to questions was stark: get vaccinated or seek a religious or medical exemption. As a non-religious person with no medical issues, I knew neither exemption applied to me.

With no other recourse, I sought out my squadron commander. I walked into his office, asking if he had a moment to discuss the vaccine. His expression told me he sensed what was coming. He closed the door, sat down, and paused—a heavy silence signaling the weight of the conversation ahead. I explained my discomfort with the vaccine, my observations of its ineffectiveness, and my ineligibility for exemptions.

What made this feel so clearly unlawful to me wasn't just policy—it was visceral. A moral alarm went off in my gut the moment the mandate was issued. I had already worked 17 months at the height of the pandemic, leading spacelift operations that kept Vandenberg Space Force Base fully functional without a single COVID infection. I had done my job safely and effectively without the vaccine. The notion that I now "posed a risk" to my vaccinated peers was not only absurd—it was dishonest. I had seen colleagues who were voluntarily vaccinated catch COVID multiple times. If the vaccine didn't stop transmission or infection, then what exactly was it protecting us from? And how could it be justified to punish those who chose to opt out? Add to that the fact that the vaccine was developed in record time with zero long-term data and no answers from leadership when I raised these concerns—it became impossible for me to comply. It wasn't just a disagreement; it felt like a lie I was being ordered to live.

I asked if there were any alternatives, even voluntary separation. He promised to make calls and get back to me. The next day, he summoned me to his office, this time with the first sergeant and senior enlisted leader present. Their presence felt like a formality, a sign that options at our level were exhausted. My commander confirmed he had explored every avenue, but there was no way around the mandate. Voluntary separation wasn't an option. If I refused the vaccine, the only path forward was disciplinary action— a "paper trail" of punishments leading to a discharge board and potential separation from service within six to eight weeks, he estimated. He asked one final time if I would get the vaccine. I held firm, stating I wasn't comfortable complying but harbored no ill will toward him or the squadron. I understood his hands were tied, and this was a situation forced upon us all. As I left his office, I knew my military career was on the brink of an irreversible shift. That evening, I went home and began mentally preparing for a life beyond the Space Force—one that would secure stability for my family.

First Reprimand

On September 22, 2021, I was informed I would receive my first-ever military punishment: a Letter of Reprimand (LOR). For an officer, an LOR is a career-ender—a formal mark on your record, noted in your Officer Performance Report, that virtually guarantees no promotion when a review board examines your file. As I entered my squadron's front office, the first sergeant and senior enlisted leader greeted me. They asked if I understood the procedure for "reporting in" to receive a punishment, then escorted me to the commander's office and closed the door. Moments later, I knocked. The commander called me to enter. I reported to his desk, saluted, stood at attention, and he began reading the following:

"MEMORANDUM FOR CAPTAIN JOSHUA M. ZERMENO

FROM: 2 SLS/CC

SUBJECT: Letter of Reprimand

On or about 9 September 2021, you failed to obey a lawful order. The lawful order that was issued to you was to receive your initial dose of a Coronavirus Disease 2019 (COVID-19) vaccine with full licensure approval from the Food and Drug Administration and provide proof by 15 September 2021. You were also ordered to receive the second dose of the same vaccine and provide proof by 15 October 2021. You indicated on Attachment 1, that you failed to comply with the lawful issued order and are in violation of Article 90 of the Uniform

Code of Military Justice.

You are hereby Reprimanded! Your conduct failed to meet the expectation of a Captain, or any officer, in the USSF. A basic tenet of military discipline is to respect the chain of command. That requires not only following the lawful orders of the officers appointed over you, but accepting those orders as your mission and zealously working to accomplish the stated ends of those orders. Strict adherence to orders is the only way a military force anywhere in the world can execute its mission. It is imperative to unite effectiveness and personal readiness that you follow lawful orders issued to you. Any repetition of this behavior or any other violation may result in more severe action.

PRIVACY ACT STATEMENT. AUTHORITY: 10 U.S.C. 8013. PURPOSE. To obtain any comments or documents you desire to submit (on a voluntary basis) for consideration concerning this action. ROUTINE USES: Provides you an opportunity to submit comments or documents for consideration. If provided, the comments and documents you submit become a part of the action. DISCLOSURE: Your written acknowledgment of receipt and signature are mandatory. Any other comments or documents you provide are voluntary.

You will acknowledge receipt of this document immediately by signing below. Your signature on this document is solely for receipt purposes and is not an admission. Unless I grant you an extension, you have three (3) duty days to submit any comments or documents you wish to be considered in rebuttal. If you submit a written response, you will be informed of my final decision regarding this action within three (3) duty days. Any comments or documents you submit in rebuttal will become part of the record.

If this letter of Reprimand is sustained, it will be placed in an UIF. Submit any comments or documents you wish to be considered concerning the UIF when you respond to the Letter of Reprimand.

Signed,

2 SLS/CC"

When he finished, I signed the LOR, saluted, and left his office. As I walked back to my own office, a crushing wave of shame, failure, and uncertainty overwhelmed me. The weight of the reprimand—a scarlet letter on my record—felt like a betrayal of my years of service, yet I stood by my conviction that the mandate was unjust. The path ahead was unclear, and the looming threat of discharge cast a shadow over my future and my family's stability.

Do Not Promote

On September 28, 2021, less than a week after receiving my first LOR, my squadron commander called me to his office. He informed me we needed to meet with the SLD 30 Commander, the base commander overseeing the 30th Space Launch Delta (SLD 30), the unit responsible for space launch operations at Vandenberg. Though the purpose wasn't explicit, I knew it likely tied to my vaccine refusal and the LOR. We met at the headquarters building and checked in with the commander's staff. My squadron commander, an exceptional officer I deeply respected, had his hands tied by the COVID-19 mandate. As we waited to be called into the SLD 30 Commander's office, he made small talk— family, football, weekend plans. In a time when few stood by me regarding the vaccine, his effort to keep things human before an undoubtedly tense meeting reminded me he was one of the good ones. Soon, we were called into the SLD 30 Commander's office. I reported in, saluted, and took a seat beside my squadron commander as directed. The SLD 30 Commander got straight to the point: this meeting was about my promotion board. He slid my promotion recommendation across the desk for me to review, explaining its contents as I read:

"Unit Mission Description:

Executes evaluation & launch in support of National Security Space Launch & Commercial Launch programs. Maintains, handles, & transports "Minotaur" small spacelift vehicles to support responsive operational capabilities at 4 continental United States locations. Provides recovery & mission integration for X-37B Orbital Test Vehicle to ensure 365-day Western Range readiness. Manages National Security Space Launch new entrant launch pad certification & maintains 7 vital spacelift processing facilities.

Job Description:

Flight commander for 18 space professionals leading resource protection, mission assurance & technical analysis for emerging launch capabilities. Executes on-console procedures with mission team during testing, range integration rehearsals & day of launch countdown. Leads launch complex oversight for SMC New Entrant Certification; validates launch providers meet critical National Security Space Launch requirements. Develops & evaluates Western Range spacelift operation plans in support of POTUS directed assured access to space initiative.

Promotion Recommendation:

Excellent engineer who performs well at assigned duties; revamped training program; fixed critical manning shortfall. Capt Zermeno was reprimanded for failing to obey SECDEF order to obtain the COVID-19 vaccine; do not promote.

Overall Recommendation: DO NOT PROMOTE"

After the SLD 30 Commander finished explaining his decision, he dismissed me. His staff provided copies of the paperwork as I left the building to return to work. I climbed into my truck in the parking lot and sat there, staring at the documents. The "Do Not Promote" recommendation for my promotion board, which would have advanced me to Major and sustained my career, was now official. In less than a month since the COVID-19 vaccine mandate, I had received my first-ever punishment—a Letter of Reprimand—and now a guarantee I would not advance in rank, all for refusing a vaccine I believed was unjust. A sinking realization hit me: things were about to get much worse.

Second Reprimand

A few weeks after receiving my "Do Not Promote" recommendation, my squadron commander once again summoned me to his office. He informed me we were to meet again with the SLD 30 Commander. This time, I had advance notice of the purpose: to receive a second LOR, delivered directly by the SLD 30 Commander. With a few days to prepare, I ensured my service dress was ready and steeled myself for what was coming. On October 25, 2021, my squadron commander and I stood outside the SLD 30 Commander's office, engaging in small talk about life—family, plans, the everyday. Looking back, I deeply appreciated his effort to keep things human before another difficult moment. He remained one of the few who had my back during the vaccine mandate ordeal. Soon, I was directed to report in. I knocked on the door, waited for permission to enter, marched to the desk, saluted, stood at attention, and listened as the SLD 30 Commander read my second Letter of Reprimand:

"MEMORANDUM FOR CAPTAIN JOSHUA M. ZERMENO

FROM: SLD 30/CC

SUBJECT: Letter of Reprimand

On or about 12 October 2021, you failed to obey a lawful order. The lawful order that was issued to you was to receive your initial dose of a Coronavirus Disease 2019 (COVID-19) vaccine with full licensure approval from the Food and Drug Administration and provide proof by 13 October 2021. You were also ordered to receive the second dose of the same vaccine and provide proof by 2 November 2021. You indicated on Attachment 1, that you failed to comply with the lawful issued order and are in violation of Article 92 of the Uniform Code of Military Justice.

You are hereby Reprimanded! Your conduct failed to meet the expectations of a commissioned officer in the USSF. A basic tenet of military discipline is to respect the chain of command. That requires not only following the lawful orders of the officers appointed over you, but accepting those orders as your mission and zealously working to accomplish it. You were previously ordered to receive your initial dose of the COVID-19 vaccine on 9 September 2021, in which you failed to follow that lawful order and received a letter of reprimand from the 2d Space Launch Squadron (2 SLS) commander. Strict adherence to orders is the only way a military force anywhere in the world can execute its mission. Continued repetition of this behavior or any other violation may result in more severe action.

PRIVACY ACT STATEMENT. AUTHORITY: 10 U.S.C. 8013. PURPOSE: To obtain any comments or documents you desire to submit (on a voluntary basis) for consideration concerning this action. ROUTINE USES: Provides you an opportunity to submit comments or documents for consideration. If provided, the comments and documents you submit become a part of the action. DISCLOSURE. Your written acknowledgment of receipt and signature are mandatory. Any other comments or documents you provide are voluntary.

You will acknowledge receipt of this document immediately by signing below. Your signature on this document is solely for receipt purposes and is not an admission. Unless I grant you an extension, you have three (3) duty days to submit any comments or documents you wish to be considered in rebuttal. If you submit a written response, you will be informed of my final decision regarding this action within three (3) duty days. Any comments or documents you submit in rebuttal will become part of the record.

If this letter of Reprimand is sustained, it will be placed in an Unfavorable Information File (UIF). Submit any comments or documents you wish to be considered concerning the UIF when you respond to the Letter of Reprimand.

Signed,

SLD 30/CC"

When he finished, I signed the document as required, saluted, and exited the office to collect a copy of the paperwork from his staff. Once again, I found myself sitting in my truck in the headquarters parking lot, staring at this new form of punishment. A creeping doubt gnawed at me—had my gut-driven decision to refuse the vaccine, which I believed to be unjust, been a mistake? The mounting consequences threatened not only my career but my family's stability. With each passing day, that fear grew heavier, casting a shadow over everything I had worked for.

Voluntary Separation?

On October 26, 2021, the day after receiving my second Letter of Reprimand from the SLD 30 Commander for refusing the COVID-19 vaccine, my first sergeant poked her head into my office. "Have you heard the news?" she asked. I hadn't, and I pressed her for details. She explained that the Department of the Air Force had released new guidance for military members refusing the vaccine, titled "20211012_Mandatory COVID-19 Vaccine FAQ." The guidance offered an administrative option for voluntary separation with commander approval. A wave of relief washed over me, and I asked her to send me a copy. She agreed, adding that she'd brief our squadron commander on the details. As I read the guidance, an even stronger sense of hope surged when I reached section 2:

"In order to retire or separate in lieu of taking the COVID-19 vaccine, regular [or active component] Active Duty airman and Guardians must have a commander-approved submission prior to 1 November 2021, and the approved retirement or separation date must be no later than 1 April 2022 (the first day of the fifth month following the COVID-19 mandatory vaccination date of 2 November 2021). If a member does not have an approved effective retirement or separation date in line with the aforementioned timelines, they are required to be vaccinated"

In simple terms, if my squadron commander approved my voluntary separation, I could leave the service, put this ordeal behind me, and move forward with my life.

Soon after, my first sergeant returned, a smile on her face. "The boss is on board," she said. "Let's go talk to him." I leapt from my chair, and we headed to the squadron commander's office. His smile mirrored hers—a clear sign this guidance was a relief for us all. He dove into the conversation, asking if I had read the guidance. "Yes, sir," I replied. "Are you sure this is the route you want to take?" he asked. With a smile of my own, I answered, "Yes, sir." He nodded, confirming he would support my voluntary separation package. I stood, shook his hand, and returned to my office to complete my portion of the application that same day.

On October 26, 2021, I initiated my voluntary separation package in lieu of receiving the COVID-19 vaccine through the online application process established by the Department of the Air Force, which also served the Space Force. For my portion of the application, I submitted the following statement:

"I will not be taking the COVID-19 vaccine, and will not be applying for a medical or religious exemption waiver. I am requesting separation from active duty service in lieu of taking the COVID-19 vaccine in accordance with section 2 of the 20211012_DAF_Mandatory COVID-19 guidance which states:

'In order to retire or separate in lieu of taking the COVID-19 vaccine, regular [or active component] Active Duty Airmen and Guardians must have a commander-approved submission prior to 1 November 2021, and the approved retirement or separation date must be no later than 1 April 2022 (the first day of the fifth month following the COVID-19 mandatory vaccination date of 2 November 2021). If a member does not have an approved effective retirement or separation date in line with the aforementioned timelines, they are required to be vaccinated.'"

Once I completed my portion, I submitted the application and notified my squadron commander that it was now in his possession. Without hesitation, he logged into his computer, checked his notifications, and confirmed receipt of the application. "I'll take care of it," he said, and immediately began his part. For his portion, he submitted the following statement:

29

"Answered 'Yes' on recent misconduct due to Capt Zermeno's failure to obey a lawful order and receive his COVID-19 vaccine. I recommend approval of this separation and waiver of his ADSC. This application follows the DAF Guidance FAQs allowing Airmen who will not receive the vaccine to apply for separation by 1 Nov 2021.

Commander Recommendation: Recommend Approval."

His prompt action—pausing his work to complete my application within an hour—was another small but meaningful gesture that underscored his care for his people and his support for me. It joined the handful of positive moments I cherished amid this ordeal.

With my squadron commander's portion complete, the application moved to his superior, the SLD 30 Commander. This was the same commander who had issued my second LOR and recommended "Do Not Promote" on my promotion board, casting a shadow of uncertainty over the application's fate. On October 29, 2021, the SLD 30 Commander submitted his comments and recommendation on my voluntary separation package:

"There is not a compelling reason to waive the ADSC to allow separation given the factors involved in this case.

Wing Commander Recommendation: Recommend Disapproval."

Just like that, my hopes of ending this ordeal were crushed, with no clear justification. I wanted to believe the SLD 30 Commander didn't grasp the devastating impact of his decision, as if I were a stranger he'd never met. But I couldn't. Days earlier, he had issued my second LOR. Weeks before that, he had recommended "Do Not Promote" on my promotion board. He knew full well my officer career was being dismantled beyond repair.

Instead of acknowledging the Department of the Air Force's guidance allowing voluntary separation in lieu of the COVID-19 vaccine—or supporting my squadron commander's recommendation for approval—he chose to deepen the spiral of punishments. The decision felt deeply personal, like a deliberate strike against my refusal to comply.

Soon after the SLD 30 Commander disapproved my application, my squadron commander called me into his office. The expression on his face was hard to read, a mix of shock, confusion, and disappointment. He had followed Air Force guidance, provided a supportive recommendation, and watched it be dismissed by his superior without explanation.

After a quiet moment, he apologized, saying he couldn't fathom the reasoning behind the decision. He offered a glimmer of hope: the disapproval wasn't final. The Secretary of the Air Force Personnel Council could still approve the application. But as I left his office, the weight of uncertainty settled heavier than ever.

The Order to Disappear

On November 2, 2021, I had just settled into my office when my squadron commander knocked and poked his head in. After a quick "good morning," he said, "I think I know the answer, but I have to ask—are you getting the shot?" I replied, "No, sir." His response was immediate: "Pack up your stuff and vacate the building. Telework until further notice." Caught off guard, I asked, "Are you serious?" He nodded, his face a mix of frustration and apology, confirming this was the latest order from leadership. I said, "Copy all, sir. I'll keep my phone and computer on me if you need anything," and began packing what I needed. As I walked out of the building, the weight of my peers' stares followed me through the "cubicle farm." No one spoke, their silence louder than words. What should have felt like a walk of shame—my final moment in the office with my team—didn't. Deep in my gut, I knew something was wrong with this situation, and I clung to that conviction as I reached my truck and drove home.

At home, I set up at my desk, powered on my computer, and kept my phone nearby in case orders changed or work called me back. The isolation felt eerily reminiscent of March 2020, when the pandemic began, but this time, I was alone in my exile. Before long, my commander reached out with guidance for the foreseeable future: stay logged into our chat system, complete administrative tasks like enlisted and officer performance reports, awards packages, and mission data reviews, dial into daily and weekly meetings by phone while others attended in person, and maintain physical fitness at home. This became my new routine—one that would define the remainder of my military career.

Isolation

By November 2021, I was isolated from my peers to the fullest extent possible. The stated reason for my exclusion: as an unvaccinated officer, I posed a risk to the vaccinated personnel at Vandenberg Space Force Base, and the military needed to protect them to maintain mission readiness. Yes, the vaccinated needed protection from me—a healthy, capable officer who had performed flawlessly throughout the COVID-19 pandemic.

"Isolation" meant professional exile. I could still live with my family, visit neighbors, shop and dine in town, and even travel with my commander's approval. But I was barred from interacting with my peers, entering government buildings, or continuing the job I had excelled at from the pandemic's onset until November 2, 2021. Despite my proven ability and perfect health, I was stripped of the chance to do my duty to the best of my abilities. This routine—teleworking in solitude, disconnected from my team—began that day and persisted through all of 2022 and nearly all of 2023, until my eventual separation from the Space Force.

Officer Performance Report

In December 2021, I received my first Officer Performance Report (OPR)—the annual performance review for officers—since the punishments for my COVID-19 vaccine refusal began. Uncertain of what to expect from my squadron commander and his superior, the SLD 30 Commander, I braced for the outcome. On one hand, I had performed my duties flawlessly until the Secretary of Defense's vaccine mandate on August 24, 2021. On the other, I had endured two LORs, a "Do Not Promote" recommendation, and expulsion from government buildings for refusing the vaccine. When I reviewed my OPR, its contents were startling:

"JOB DESCRIPTION:

Oversees 97 Airmen tasked with transport, test and launch support to Delta, Falcon 9, Minotaur I/IV and X-37 program missions. Supports sole USSF expeditionary space lift maintenance team; maintains $7.6 million and 535 Minotaur GSE items for cross-coast capabilities. Conducts planning and execution for $2.5M special operations projects; Oversees 7 launch facilities worth $80M. Manages end-to-end integration of space lift operations; leads evaluation and analysis of new entrants across 7 launch vehicle platforms.

RATER OVERALL ASSESSMENT:

DOES NOT MEET STANDARDS

Controlled National Security Space Launch Phase II award fee inputs; drove desired Launch Service Provider behaviors; ensured all PWS requirements were met on $3.3 billion contract. Organized eastern and western range cooperation; fixed critical manning shortfall; maximized mission coverage by cross-training 104 personnel. Managed 46-member on-console pathfinder team; developed mission assurance cross-coast standardized operation plans; Vandenberg Space Force Base ready to support SpaceX mission. Reviewed three key squadron operating instructions; captured evolving roles and responsibilities; ensured governance in step with Space Systems Command organizational changes. Natural choice for Assistant Director of Operations; augmented squadron leadership staff tackling complex projects and concerns; ready for future United States Space Force Duties. Member received 2 Letters of Reprimand from squadron commander and Space Launch Delta 30 commander for failure to obey a lawful order and refusing the COVID-19 vaccine.

ADDITIONAL RATER OVERALL ASSESSMENT:

CONCUR

Enhanced virtual reality launch engineering training; synchronized coasts and updated standards for multiple launch service provider rockets; slashed qualification time 50%. Led SpaceX post-launch evaluations; identified 11 issues and built enterprise-wide resolutions; Space Launch Delta 30 prepared for a 20X launch tempo increase. Handpicked Day-of-Launch Subject Matter Expert. Conduit between tech team and launch director for critical launch vehicle data; set continuity of National Security Space Launch missions through 2027. Comments from the ratee were requested but were not received within the required period."

In essence, my squadron commander and the SLD 30 Commander acknowledged my exceptional performance, consistent with my record over years of service. The report detailed my leadership in critical missions, proving COVID-19 had no impact on my ability to excel. Yet, they marked "DOES NOT MEET

STANDARDS" solely for refusing the COVID-19 vaccine.

This OPR became my fifth major punishment in three months for standing against the vaccine mandate, following two LORs, a "Do Not Promote" recommendation, and my exclusion from government buildings. After eleven years of unblemished service in the Air Force and Space Force, I had now accumulated enough penalties to render my career "over" in the eyes of most military leaders.

Voluntary Separation Denied

On February 3, 2022, more than three months after I applied for voluntary separation in lieu of receiving the COVID-19 vaccine—a process established by the Department of the Air Force and Space Force—I received official word that my request had been denied by the Secretary of the Air Force Personnel Council. Their statement read:

"ACTION on behalf of the SECRETARY OF THE AIR FORCE: The resignation submitted on 28 October 2021 by Captain Joshua M. Zermeno, under the provisions for miscellaneous reasons has not been accepted. The Board determined the justification submitted by the applicant did not demonstrate it was in the best interest of the Department of the Air Force and Space Force to separate early given their significant lengthy service commitment.

This action is taken under the authority delegated by the Secretary of the Air Force.

Signed,

Director, SAF Personnel Council"

I had followed the Air Force's process to the letter, meeting every requirement for voluntary separation and securing my squadron commander's approval. Yet, the higher authorities deemed my separation "not in the best interest of the Department of the Air Force and Space Force," offering no substantive explanation.

I was speechless. The hope I had clung to for three months evaporated, leaving me grappling with a single question: "What's next?" My call with my squadron commander offered no clarity. He, too, was at a loss for words. He had adhered to the Department's guidance, provided his approval, and watched it be dismissed without a valid reason.

In that moment, I sensed a shift in my commander. Though I couldn't speak for him, his demeanor suggested a mix of betrayal and frustration, as if he felt undermined by his superior, the SLD 30 Commander, and the Personnel Council's decision to ignore his recommendation. When I asked, "What's next?" he instructed me to continue teleworking as I had been, promising to find out what steps to take. But the path forward felt more uncertain than ever.

Looking back, some might ask why I didn't pursue legal action. At the time, it never felt like an option. I was repeatedly told by JAG officers and commanders that the order to receive the vaccine was lawful. Every conversation reinforced that resistance would only lead to punishment, not protection. I had zero hope the legal system would support me, and I was isolated in my belief. But now, years later, I've learned that the Department of Defense based its mandate on the availability of an FDA-approved vaccine—a claim that has since been widely challenged. Though the Pfizer-BioNTech vaccine received full FDA approval under the name "Comirnaty" on August 23, 2021, that version was never made available to service members. Instead, doses remained under Emergency Use Authorization, making the mandate legally questionable from the start. At the time, I didn't have the legal understanding or access to challenge the narrative I was fed.

UCMJ

On February 9, 2022, six days after the Secretary of the Air Force Personnel Council denied my voluntary separation request, my squadron commander and I were once again summoned to the office of the SLD 30 Commander. He announced he was considering recommending that I face punishment under Article 15 of the Uniform Code of Military Justice (UCMJ), to be administered by the Brigadier General at Space Systems Command (SSC). Having already recommended disapproval of my voluntary separation package—a process designed for service members refusing the COVID-19 vaccine—the SLD 30 Commander was now intensifying his punitive and intimidating tactics.

His malicious intent became unmistakable: a deliberate, authoritarian abuse of his command authority. I was reduced to a mere pawn in his campaign of intimidation, a stark demonstration of power meant to suppress everyone under his command at Vandenberg Space Force Base. My respect for him as a military officer vanished. The Air Force and Space Force often champion their commitment to putting people first, yet the SLD 30 Commander's actions were a blatant betrayal of that ideal. His targeted punitive measures against unvaccinated service members and their families cast a relentless shadow of retribution, with no relief in sight for those bearing the weight of his punishments.

Psychological Warfare

In early 2022, my story became a grueling waiting game, left to wonder what the Air Force and Space Force would do with me. I had made it unequivocally clear: I would not get the COVID-19 vaccine. Their intimidation tactics—two LORs, a "Do Not Promote" recommendation, expulsion from government buildings, three months of isolation from my peers, denial of my voluntary separation package, and threats of punishment under Article 15 of the UCMJ—had failed to break me. The only way the military could force the vaccine on me was through physical restraint, a possibility I contemplated daily for months, never dismissing it as out of reach.

The waiting game was psychological warfare, a calculated campaign by the command to coerce my compliance with the COVID-19 vaccine mandate. As a graduate of both the basic and advanced SERE courses for the Air Force, I recognized the hallmarks of such tactics—and the command's actions mirrored them with chilling precision. They barred me from interacting with peers to isolate me, banned me from government buildings to sever my professional purpose, and assigned menial tasks far below my rank to erode my sense of worth. By systematically dismantling my career on paper, they instilled uncertainty, leaving me without answers about what lay ahead. Each move was designed to wear down my resolve, and the undeniable toll on my family deepened the strain. This was, without question, the lowest point of my life.

How did I endure this reality? First, I anchored myself to what mattered most: my family. They depended on me, and it was my duty to provide stability amid the chaos. Forced into a long-distance marriage as we worked to secure our family's future after my isolation, my wife and I stayed connected through daily FaceTime and phone calls, committing to monthly in-person visits—a lifeline we both cherished. On base, I shielded our children from my work turmoil, striving to preserve the stable life they'd known since the pandemic's onset. Second, I coped by detaching from the broader reality, focusing on one day at a time. My routine became my anchor: waking early to exercise, eating breakfast, and getting the kids to school; checking emails and tackling tasks for a few hours; breaking for a second workout and lunch; finishing work, picking up the kids, and managing their sports, homework, and dinner; then handling chores, unwinding, and connecting with my wife via call or FaceTime before sleep. This was what I could control, and I fixed my mind on it, day after day, through 20 months of isolation.

Testing in the Apocalypse

In the early days of the DoD's COVID-19 vaccine mandate, I took my children to the 30th Medical Group at Vandenberg Space Force Base for testing, a requirement to clear them for school after a classmate's exposure. What should have been a routine visit turned into a haunting spectacle, like a scene from an apocalyptic movie. As a Space Force officer already questioning the mandate, I was on edge, but that day—watching the military's handling of testing with my children by my side—I felt a deep unease about the ethical failures I believed were unfolding, failures that would later fuel my fight for justice, though these are my personal reflections and not legal claims.

The process felt off from the start. I called the medical group to schedule a testing time and arrived with my kids as instructed. We joined a line of service members, spouses, and other children in a parking lot under a gray California sky. Tables were spaced out in the open, with no partitions, no privacy. Military personnel in uniform shouted instructions: stand at the table, take the test, wait for results. My children, nervous but trusting, held my hands as we stepped forward in a group setting, surrounded by dozens of others. There was zero privacy; everyone could see who was testing, who was waiting, who was moving.

The tests were rapid antigen swabs, with results delivered on the spot. Those who tested negative, like my children, were cleared to go home, but those who tested positive were directed to a "Positive Test Documentation Table" in full view of everyone. I watched as a young mother with her son, a boy no older than my own, was sent to the table, heads turning, eyes tracking them. There was no anonymity, no shield for their dignity. Everyone knew who tested positive, and I could imagine the rumors that would spread through base schools and the community—shaming, bullying, whispers about "that family." To me, the process felt dehumanizing, stripping away privacy and exposing people to judgment in a way that seemed like a public sentencing.

As we walked away, cleared but shaken, I couldn't shake the apocalyptic feeling. The sterile tables, the lines of people, the segregation of "positives" from "negatives"—it was like a dystopian film where rights were erased. But this was Vandenberg, and in my view, the 30th Medical Group's procedures were deeply troubling, though I'm sharing my perspective, not asserting legal violations.

From my standpoint, the setup seemed to disregard privacy by publicly exposing health information. I felt there was no informed consent, no disclosure about the rapid antigen test kits we were subjected to, which I personally believed might have been questionable in their safety and origin, potentially lacking proper oversight. In my opinion, these tests were being used in a way that went beyond their intended purpose, segregating people publicly in a manner I found unethical. For the children I saw, I worried this public identification could lead to discrimination and bullying, a risk I believe the DoD should have anticipated.

I also questioned the science behind the process. Rapid antigen tests, from what I understood, were not meant for definitive decisions, yet the 30th Medical Group used them to label and separate people, which I felt eroded trust in the military medical system for the hundreds of families who went through it. To me, it seemed like a weapon—testing as the first strike, followed by masks and jabs—designed to control, not protect.

That day left a mark. My children, spared the label of "positive," still felt the tension, asking why that boy had to go to the other table. I felt the weight of their questions, knowing I couldn't shield them from what I saw as the military's failures. But it also steeled my resolve. Together, we'd demand accountability for what I perceived as breaches of dignity, for the privacy I felt was stolen, for the humanity I believed was stripped from our families. The apocalypse I witnessed that day wasn't the end; it was the beginning of a fight that was far from over.

UCMJ Part 2

On June 1, 2022, I was notified by the Area Defense Counsel (ADC) that the Brigadier General, Deputy Commander of Space Systems Command (SSC), had initiated action against me, based on the SLD 30 Commander's recommendation submitted months earlier, under Air Force Instruction (AFI) 36-3206, Chapter 3, Paragraph 3.6.4, for Serious or Recurring Misconduct Punishable by Military or Civilian Authorities. The notification required me to show cause for retention on active duty, a formal step toward potential administrative separation.

I consulted with my legal representative at the ADC, and we reviewed the full scope of my situation. By this point, I had endured two LORs, a "Do Not Promote" recommendation, a "Does Not Meet Standards" mark on my Officer Performance Report, eight months of exclusion from government buildings at Vandenberg Space Force Base, and now faced UCMJ action from a general at SSC. My counsel advised that submitting a conditional waiver was in my best interest, and I agreed. The waiver stated I would forgo my right to an administrative discharge board hearing in exchange for a service characterization of no less than honorable. In essence, I was again trying to save time and resources by requesting voluntary separation with an honorable discharge. My reasoning was rooted in my 11 years of honorable service and my prior attempt to use the Air Force's administrative separation process for vaccine refusers—a process that had failed me, my family, and other service members. I had exhausted every effort to resolve this ordeal, hoping the Brigadier General would recognize my service and rectify the situation. I signed the waiver, my ADC team submitted it to the general for review, and I was left waiting to learn what lay ahead for my life, career, and family.

Change of Command

In June 2023, our squadron held a formal Change of Command ceremony, a time-honored military tradition where the outgoing commander transfers authority to their successor. These ceremonies, steeped in protocol and symbolism, mark a pivotal transition, often stirring a mix of emotions among service members: relief if the departing leader was ineffective, sorrow if they were exceptional, or uncertainty about the incoming commander's leadership style. I felt a profound sadness as my outgoing squadron commander prepared to depart for his next assignment. He had been a rare ally, treating me with dignity throughout the COVID-19 mandate ordeal, standing out as the one leader who supported me amid relentless punishments. Facing ongoing disciplinary actions and an uncertain future for my family, I braced for the change with trepidation.

After the ceremony, the new commander began one-on-one meetings with his leadership team to establish rapport. When my turn came, I was granted permission to enter his office for an in-person meeting—a rare exception given my eight-month ban from government buildings. I approached with cautious optimism, hoping for a fresh perspective. But the conversation quickly turned to my vaccine refusal. "I've been briefed on your situation, and I'm tracking your stance," he said, before stating it was his duty to recommend I get vaccinated and informing me of resources touting the vaccine's safety and efficacy. I firmly reiterated my position: nothing the military did would convince me to take the COVID-19 shot. As I left, his rigid focus on documentation and rules gave off a "yes man" demeanor, suggesting a lack of the experience or empathy needed to genuinely care for his people. I walked away with diminished respect for his leadership and dwindling hope for my career and family's stability.

In the months that followed, the new commander intensified efforts to pressure unvaccinated service members. He mandated weekly COVID-19 testing in public settings—sick or not—sought alternative ways to discipline those who resisted, and sent regular emails warning members not to "continue down this path." His actions made one thing clear: he would not be an ally for the rest of my time in service.

UCMJ Part 3

On September 6, 2022, I received the Brigadier General's response to my conditional waiver, a pivotal moment in my battle against the COVID-19 vaccine mandate. The Deputy Commander of SSC, acting on the SLD 30 Commander's earlier recommendation, delivered his decision:

"On 1 June 2022, I initiated action against you under AFI 36-3206, Chapter 3, paragraph 3.6.4, Serious or Recurring Misconduct Punishable by Military or Civilian Authorities, that required you to show cause for retention on active duty. On 16 June 2022, you responded with a conditional waiver of your administrative discharge board hearing rights contingent on receipt of no less than an honorable service characterization.

Having carefully considered your offer, I reject your conditional waiver. While I still intend to recommend your separation with an honorable service characterization, I am unwilling to so limit the Secretary of the Air Force's characterization options. Were he to reject your conditional waiver, we would be back in this same place many months from now, which is not good for you or the Department of the Air Force. Thus, I am advising you that either an unconditional waiver must be submitted or a board hearing will be scheduled. If you fail to respond within 3 workdays or by the end of an extension approved by 2 SLS/CC, a board hearing will be convened."

The rejection hit hard, another escalation in a campaign that had already cost me two LORs, a "Do Not Promote" recommendation, a negative OPR, and over ten months of exclusion from government buildings. After consulting my ADC, I made my stand that same day: I asserted my right to an administrative discharge board. If the Brigadier General or the Secretary of the Air Force refused to grant me an honorable discharge for my 11 years of exemplary service—despite my application for the Department of the Air Force's administrative discharge process, which had my squadron commander's approval but was denied, leaving me no way out—they would have to justify it before a board of my peers, scrutinizing my entire career. I was done yielding to their pressure. With my family's future and my dignity at stake, I steeled myself for a prolonged fight, committed to seeing it through to the end.

Intimidation by Testing

When my new commander took over, I hoped for a reprieve from the relentless pressure I faced as an unvaccinated Space Force officer. Instead, I found myself confronting a new form of intimidation, one wielded through mandatory squadron testing that felt more like a public shaming than a health measure. Already banned from government buildings since November 2021, I was isolated from my peers, but this new tactic brought the fight directly to me, testing my resolve in a way that cut deeper than I expected.

The commander ordered all unvaccinated members, including me, to undergo weekly COVID-19 testing—whether we were sick or not. These weren't tests conducted by the 30th Medical Group with medical staff; they were run by squadron personnel, often in a public setting on base, with everyone watching. I couldn't even step inside government buildings due to my ban, so there was no operational reason to test me. In my view, the intent was unmistakable: to intimidate, shame, and pressure us into compliance with the vaccine mandate. The setup reminded me of the unsettling testing I'd witnessed with my children at the 30th Medical Group—zero privacy, all eyes on us—but unlike that experience, which tested everyone regardless of their choices, this felt like a deliberate tactic to single us out as unvaccinated members and make us feel like outcasts. To me, it was a stark reminder of what I saw as the military's broader failures, a system that seemed more focused on control than protection, though this reflects my personal perspective.

I refused to comply with this charade. I informed my commander I'd continue testing as I had since the pandemic began: if I was sick or had symptoms, I'd get checked out properly. But I wouldn't submit to public testing, and I wouldn't show up to test if I wasn't sick. After missing a couple of these mandatory tests, I received harsh warnings: follow orders, or face further punishments. I held firm, telling him my stance wouldn't change. The tests were rapid antigen swabs, the same tools I'd seen before, which I believed were unreliable for making definitive decisions based on my understanding of their limitations. Yet my squadron used them to label and control, which I felt eroded trust in the chain of command for those of us who stood our ground.

My defiance didn't go unnoticed. While I didn't receive official paperwork for refusing, the issue was raised during my discharge board preparations, driven by the Brigadier General at SSC. I was told it would be used against me as an example of refusing to obey lawful orders. Each missed test became a mark against my character, a supposed stain on my 12-year career of flawless service. I braced myself, knowing the consequences could be severe, but I couldn't back down—not when the principle was so clear, not when I viewed the military's tactics as unjust.

The squadron's testing mirrored what I saw as broader failures in the DoD's pandemic response. I felt there was no informed consent, no disclosure about the rapid antigen test kits we were subjected to, which I personally questioned for their safety and origin, believing they might lack proper oversight. To me, they were being used to segregate and shame us in a way that felt like an overreach, though I'm sharing my perspective, not asserting legal violations. In my opinion, it seemed like a weapon—testing as the first strike, followed by masks and jabs—designed to control, not protect.

That experience with my new commander deepened the sting of isolation I already felt. I'd been labeled a criminal for my moral stand, but this public testing pushed me further, testing my resolve in a way that felt deeply personal. It wasn't just about me—it was about the principle, about the dignity of every service member forced to endure such tactics. I thought of my children, of the questions they'd asked during our own testing ordeal, and knew I had to keep fighting. I couldn't shield them from what I saw as the military's failures, but I could fight for a system that wouldn't punish us for standing our ground. Together, we'd demand accountability for what I perceived as breaches of dignity, for the privacy I felt was stolen, for the humanity I believed was stripped from us all. The intimidation I faced wasn't the end; it was fuel for a fight that was far from over.

The Waiting War

In the fall of 2022, after asserting my right to an administrative discharge board to have my career and punishments scrutinized before a panel of officers, I was thrust back into a grueling waiting game. The Brigadier General at SSC, acting on the SLD 30 Commander's recommendation, had rejected my conditional waiver in September, leaving me with no set date for the board hearing. The delay felt deliberate, a tactic to erode my resolve. Meetings with my ADC to gather career documents and peer statements offered fleeting purpose, but the ongoing intimidation from my squadron commander— forced public COVID-19 testing for the unvaccinated, menial tasks far below my rank, and isolation from my peers—compounded the strain. Another career-damaging Officer Performance Report loomed, marking over a year of relentless punishments for refusing the COVID-19 vaccine, with no end in sight.

The Space Force's tactics echoed the psychological warfare I'd recognized through my SERE training. As my family and I faced our second holiday season under this oppressive shadow, the festive warmth of Thanksgiving and Christmas clashed with leadership's calculated efforts to isolate and demoralize me for my stance. Drawing on SERE strategies, I narrowed my world to what I could control: daily routines, family moments, and mental fortitude. Above all, my family remained my anchor. Their reliance on me fueled my resolve to endure, no matter how long the fight persisted.

Mandate Rescinded

On January 10, 2023, days before my administrative discharge board was set to convene, my ADC team delivered monumental news: Secretary of Defense Lloyd Austin had issued a memorandum rescinding the COVID-19 vaccination requirements for the armed forces. The memo read:

"Subject: Rescission of August 24, 2021 and November 30, 2021 Coronavirus Disease 2019 Vaccination Requirements for Members of the Armed Forces

I am deeply proud of the Department's work to combat the coronavirus disease 2019 (COVID-19). Through your leadership, we have improved the health of our Service members and the readiness of the Force, and we have provided life-saving assistance to the American people and surged support to local health care systems and agencies at all levels of government. The Department has helped ensure the vaccination of many Americans, while simultaneously providing critical and timely acquisition support for life-saving therapeutics, tests, and treatments for COVID-19. We have demonstrated the ability to support and defend the Nation under the most trying circumstances.

The Department will continue to promote and encourage COVID-19 vaccination for all Service members. The Department has made COVID-19 vaccination as easy and convenient as possible, resulting in vaccines administered to over two million Service members and 96 percent of the Force – Active and Reserve – being fully vaccinated. Vaccination enhances operational readiness and protects the Force. All commanders have the responsibility and authority to preserve the Department's compelling interests in mission accomplishment. This responsibility and authority includes the ability to maintain military readiness, unit cohesion, good order and discipline, and the health and safety of a resilient Joint Force.

On December 23, 2022 the James M. Inhofe National Defense Authorization Act (NDAA) for Fiscal Year (FY) 2023 was enacted. Section 525 of the NDAA for FY 2023 requires me to rescind the mandate that members of the Armed Forces be vaccinated against COVID-19, issued in my August 24, 2021 memorandum, "Mandatory Coronavirus Disease 2019 Vaccination of Department of Defense Service Members." I hereby rescind that memorandum. I also hereby rescind my November 30, 2021 memorandum, "Coronavirus Disease 2019 Vaccination for Members of the National Guard and the Ready Reserve".

No individuals currently serving in the Armed Forces shall be separated solely on the basis of their refusal to receive the COVID-19 vaccination if they sought an accommodation on religious, administrative, or medical grounds. The Military Departments will update the records of such individuals to remove any adverse actions solely associated with denials of such requests, including letters of reprimand. The Secretaries of the Military Departments will further cease any ongoing reviews of current Service member religious, administrative, or medical accommodation requests solely for exemption from the COVID-19 vaccine or appeals of denials of such requests.

Religious liberty is a foundational principle of enduring importance in America, enshrined in our Constitution and other sources of Federal law. Service members have the right to observe the tenets of their religion or to observe no religion at all, as provided in applicable Federal law and Departmental policy. Components shall continue to apply the uniform standards set forth in DoD Instruction 1300.17, "Religious Liberty in the Military Services."

Other standing Departmental policies, procedures, and processes regarding immunizations remain in effect. These include the ability of commanders to consider, as appropriate, the individual immunization status of personnel in making deployment, assignment, and other operational decisions, including when vaccination is required for travel to, or entry into, a foreign nation.

For Service members administratively discharged on the sole basis that the Service member failed to obey a lawful order to receive a vaccine for COVID-19, the Department is precluded by law from awarding any characterization less than a general (under honorable conditions) discharge. Former Service members may petition their Military Department's Discharge Review Boards and Boards for Correction of Military or Naval Records to individually request a correction to their personnel records, including records regarding the characterization of their discharge.

The Under Secretary of Defense for Personnel and Readiness shall issue additional guidance to ensure uniform implementation of this memorandum, as appropriate.

The Department's COVID-19 vaccination efforts will leave a lasting legacy in the many lives we saved, the world-class Force we have been able to field, and the high level of readiness we have maintained, amidst difficult public health conditions. Our efforts were possible due, first and foremost, to the strength and dedication of our people. I remain profoundly grateful to the men and women of the Department of Defense for their efforts to protect our Force, the Department of Defense community, and to aid the American people.

Signed,

Secretary of Defense, Lloyd Austin"

Relief surged through me as I read the memo. After 16 months of relentless punishments for refusing the COVID-19 vaccine, I saw a glimmer of hope on the horizon. The memo's pivotal statement fueled my hope:

"No individuals currently serving in the Armed Forces shall be separated solely on the basis of their refusal to receive the COVID-19 vaccination if they sought an accommodation on religious, administrative, or medical grounds. The Military Departments will update the records of such individuals to remove any adverse actions solely associated with denials of such requests, including letters of reprimand."

My November 2021 application for the Department of the Air Force's voluntary separation program placed me within this protection. My reprimands, promotion denials, and negative OPRs, all tied to vaccine refusal, could be expunged, potentially reviving my career.

I met with my squadron commander and first sergeant to initiate record corrections, and they assured me they would ensure compliance. Days later, my ADC team confirmed the Board of Inquiry was canceled, halting an 11-month saga of paperwork, isolation from peers, and family strain. My attorney's voice brimmed with relief and triumph, as if we'd conquered a grueling battle. For a fleeting moment, I shared his elation, daring to believe the worst was behind me, though the path to full restoration remained uncertain.

Do Not Promote Part 2

In early 2023, after the COVID-19 vaccine mandates were rescinded, my discharge board canceled, and my records ordered corrected, I let my guard down, believing the worst was behind me. I was gravely mistaken. Not long after, my squadron commander summoned me to his office and delivered a gut punch: I had been passed over for promotion to Major a second time, triggering involuntary separation for failure to promote. Unlike the year prior, when I was called into the SLD 30 Commander's office for notification and provided a clear paperwork trail, I was neither included in meetings nor given any documentation for this "Do Not Promote" recommendation. The process was shrouded in secrecy, with minimal transparency to justify it.

Stunned, I pressed my commander for answers. How could this happen when my records—tainted solely by my refusal to take the COVID-19 vaccine—were supposed to be corrected per Secretary of Defense Lloyd Austin's January 2023 memorandum? He offered no clarity, only a vague, "We'll look into it, but I'd prepare for separation. Record corrections could take months." In that moment, the truth hit hard: the Department of Defense wasn't done punishing me. Far from being in the clear, I faced a cunning maneuver—an involuntary separation disguised as unrelated to my vaccine refusal, yet rooted in the same vendetta. My 12 years of service teetered on the edge, and the battle was far from over.

Failure to Correct Records

In early 2023, weeks after the second "Do Not Promote" recommendation triggered my involuntary separation , I clung to the hope that my records would be corrected as mandated by Secretary of Defense Lloyd Austin's January 2023 memorandum. That hope crumbled when my squadron commander called with an update. While my punishments could be removed from my UIF, he had no clear guidance on how to make it happen for my tainted OPRS or promotion recommendations in time to halt my separation. The only option, he said, was a board review process that could take up to a year. I could submit documentation, proceed with separation, and—if the board eventually corrected my records—potentially return to service.

The proposal was a logistical nightmare. As a husband and father of six, I couldn't uproot my family or couch-surf for a year while awaiting an uncertain outcome. Stability for my wife and children was non-negotiable. Shock turned to indignation as I realized the stark contrast: my chain of command had swiftly issued career-ending punishments when the COVID-19 vaccine mandate was enforced, yet showed no urgency to comply with its rescission and save my career. Their failure to correct my records in a timely manner wasn't just negligence—it was a betrayal. By pushing me toward involuntary separation with only a faint promise of future reinstatement, they severed the last thread of trust I had in them. My 12 years of service, and my family's future, were left in limbo.

Involuntary Separation

In the spring of 2023, as my involuntary separation from the United States Space Force loomed, I faced a grueling preparation process, holding onto a dwindling hope that my chain of command would correct my records and stop the separation. The second "Do Not Promote" recommendation, a direct result of my refusal to take the COVID-19 vaccine, had set this in motion, despite Secretary of Defense Lloyd Austin's January 2023 memorandum mandating the correction of such punitive records. Yet, as weeks turned to months, no salvation arrived.

On the military side, I tackled a series of administrative tasks. I enrolled in the Transition Assistance Program (TAP), a mandatory week-long course on civilian life, covering resume crafting, job hunting, and VA benefits. The sessions felt hollow, like planning a future I hadn't chosen. Out-processing was a draining checklist: I returned equipment, completed medical evaluations, and attended my security clearance outbrief. I arranged terminal leave which was used for concentrating on setting up a civilian life for my family and I. Each task chipped away at my 13 years of service, reducing my career to bureaucratic formalities.

On the personal front, the challenges were crushing. As a husband and father of six, I poured hours into job applications, targeting roles in aerospace, logistics, and program management to leverage my military expertise. But two years of relentless punishments—Letters of Reprimand, referral Officer Performance Reports, and promotion denials—had shredded my professional reputation, tainted my records, and derailed my career. Employers saw gaps and red flags, not the dedicated officer I was. Rejections mounted, and interviews were rare, intensifying the pressure to secure stable income. Finding housing for a family of eight was equally harrowing. We scoured listings across California and beyond, prioritizing school districts and potential job locations, all while wrestling with the uncertainty of our next chapter. Every application and house hunt was a desperate bid to anchor my wife and children in a stable future.

Despite these efforts, I clung to a faint hope that my chain of command would act—that the SLD 30 Commander or squadron leadership would correct my records, as mandated, and halt the separation. But their inaction was deafening. The same leaders who had swiftly enforced career-ending punishments in 2021 showed no urgency to undo the damage. Time slipped away, and on August 31, 2023, I was involuntarily separated from the Space Force after 13 years of service. The official reason—failure to promote—veiled the truth: my refusal to comply with the COVID-19 vaccine mandate. My career, and my family's security, were casualties of an unrelenting vendetta. With my career officially over, the civilian world awaited—a new battleground where my family and I would face challenges we never anticipated.

Impact on Family

Picture a family standing at the edge of a dream—a new home purchased for a fresh start, children laughing in unfamiliar rooms, a future that finally feels free from uncertainty. Now picture it crumbling: a husband and wife torn apart, a premature baby fighting for breath, five children caught in a storm of instability. This was my family's story—and it echoed the experience of thousands of military families shattered by the COVID-19 vaccine mandate between August 2021 and August 2023.

If you've paused to imagine our pain, you carry the empathy of a true leader. If you haven't—and you hold power over others—stop and ask yourself: Do your decisions lift up those you lead, or do they shatter the lives you'll never see? Leadership isn't just policy—it's the ripple that can save or destroy families like mine. The mandate's enforcers chose destruction, and their betrayal cut deeper than any order, leaving a nation of military families to claw their way back from ruin.

In 2021, I stood at a crossroads. Leadership at Vandenberg Space Force Base warned I'd be discharged for refusing the vaccine, a mandate I believed— deep in my gut—was not just wrong but unlawful. After applying for the Air Force's voluntary separation, my wife and I took a leap of faith, buying an out-of-state home to anchor our children's future. But when the separation was denied, our dream became a trap. For nine months, we lived apart—she in our new home with her two children, I in California with my three—our family cleaved by the mandate's chaos. Determined to keep our marriage strong, we committed to seeing each other once a month, meeting halfway or flying across states for a weekend at a time. With children in tow, we packed bags, coordinated flights, arranged childcare, and navigated long drives—often spending more time on the road than we had together. Each reunion was a lifeline—but it was also a reminder of what we were missing. We clung to those weekends, trying to stitch together the frayed fabric of our marriage with just 48 hours of togetherness before the next painful goodbye. The strain took its toll. In July 2022, during a brief visit to California, my wife—pregnant and overwhelmed—woke in excruciating pain. At just 24 weeks, she gave birth to Constance Murphy, our 1-pound-8-ounce miracle, who was rushed first to Santa Barbara's NICU and then to Cedars-Sinai in Los Angeles for a gauntlet of life-saving procedures—fighting through brain bleeds, heart surgeries, and months of fragile, uncertain hope.

Our five other children, caught in the mandate's fallout, were uprooted between states and schools, their lives a revolving door of instability that a 2021 separation could have spared. We burned through our savings trying to keep our family home, then abandoned it to relocate my wife and stepchildren to California for Constance's care. The distance and despair pushed our marriage to the edge, each call a battle to hold our bond together. What we'd built—a family united by love and plans—was reduced to financial ruin and emotional wreckage, our unity fractured by a mandate that cared nothing for the lives it upended. And we were not alone. Thousands of military families faced their own versions of this pain—homes lost, marriages strained, children's futures stolen—because leaders chose compliance over compassion.

As a husband and father of six, I put my family first, above my role as a service member. I forced a smile to shield my children, standing resolute against a mandate I saw as a violation of principle. But the cost was steep. My chain of command offered only token gestures—meal trains from spouses, 2-minute calls from the commander, the kind any new parent gets, not the support we needed for our mandate-driven struggles. They didn't care about my wife's recovery, our children's turmoil, or Constance's fight. Vaccine punishments were their focus, a relentless pressure that shadowed us until my career ended.

Three years later, Constance is a walking, talking miracle, a light in every room. But our family bears scars no time can erase. We ask ourselves: If the mandate's stress hadn't gripped my wife, would Constance have been born whole, spared those desperate surgeries? Would our five other children have the stable home we fought for? The mandate didn't just take my career—it stole our future, and the futures of thousands, leaving us to rebuild from the ashes.

A Father's Shield

As the Department of Defense's COVID-19 vaccine mandate tore through my career from 2021 to 2023, I faced a battle far harder than any reprimand or isolation: shielding my children from the storm I knew would upend their world. I had always been their steady hand—the father who made lunches, coached their sports, and launched the rockets at Vandenberg Space Force Base that lit up the sky, missions I'd led with pride as a Space Force officer. But as the mandate's punishments mounted, I became a master of deflection, hiding the truth to protect their innocence, even as the weight of that facade carved a hollow space inside me.

I kept my work details as private as possible, a stark contrast to the years when my children had been part of my military life. They'd loved "bring your kid to work" days—exploring my office, touring launch sites to see the Falcon 9 rocket, visiting the base museum, and building small rockets themselves. But after I was banned from government buildings in November 2021, those days were gone. When they asked about the next event, their eyes bright with anticipation, I forced a smile and said, "They had to cancel them because of COVID." It was a half-truth that stung, knowing the real reason was my refusal to comply with an order I believed was unlawful. When they asked when my next rocket launch was, I'd say, "I'm working on new projects that'll launch in the future," a vague promise to mask the fact that I'd been stripped of my role in those missions I'd once led. When they wondered why I was working from home, I told them, "I'm on special projects assigned just to me," hoping they'd imagine something exciting instead of the menial tasks I was relegated to in exile.

The hardest lies came when our family's future hung in the balance. In 2021, after applying for voluntary separation, my wife and I bought an out-of-state home to anchor our children's future, a dream we thought would bring stability. But when the separation was denied, we were stuck living apart—me in California with my three, her in the new home with her two, our youngest, Constance, born prematurely amid the chaos. The kids kept asking, "When are we moving?" I'd reply, "It's up to the military, out of our hands," hiding the bitter truth that the military's vendetta against me had fractured our plans. When my involuntary separation came in August 2023, they asked if I'd have a going-away party, like the ones they'd attended for others over the years—joyful events with cake, speeches, and laughter. I swallowed hard and said, "We can't have one because of COVID," another excuse to shield them from the reality that their father had been cast out, branded a criminal for standing on principle. Those experiences they'd loved—launch days, base events, a sense of military family—were stolen from them, just as my career was stolen from me. I was left making excuses, each one a brick in the wall I built to protect them.

The emotional toll of this facade was crushing. Every forced smile, every vague answer, carried a pang of guilt—I wasn't being fully honest with the children I'd sworn to guide with integrity. I feared they'd sense my pain, that my strained laughter or distant gaze would betray the turmoil I hid. One evening in early 2022, as I tucked my youngest son into bed after a day of teleworking in isolation, he looked up and asked, "Dad, why don't you wear your uniform anymore?" The question hit like a gut punch, his innocent curiosity slicing through my defenses. I froze, then forced a gentle smile. "I'm working on special projects from home, buddy," I said, ruffling his hair. "Uniforms are for the base, but I'm still your dad, right here for you." He nodded, satisfied, but I turned away, my throat tight, knowing I'd dodged the truth to preserve his sense of security.

That moment, and so many like it, is why I wrote this memoir. As I said in the beginning, one day my children will ask why I made the choices I did. This is the story I'll tell them—not just of the mandate's betrayal, but of the father who fought to shield them, even when it broke him inside. I wanted them to hold onto their childhood a little longer, to believe in a world where their dad was still their hero, even as that world tried to tear me down.

The Civilian Transition

When I was involuntarily separated from the United States Space Force on August 31, 2023, after 13 years of service, I stepped into a civilian world that stripped my family and me to nothing—a hollow shell of the life we'd built. The DoD's COVID-19 vaccine mandate had already branded me a criminal, tainting my record with LORs, referral OPRs, and promotion denials. Now, my wife and I faced the wreckage alone, just the two of us against the world, with no support network on base to lean on, though a few family members sent what funds they were able to help us out. The months that followed tore us down to our core, but in that desolation, we found what truly mattered: each other.

The job hunt was a soul-crushing ordeal. I applied for dozens of jobs over months, targeting roles in aerospace and logistics where my military expertise should have shone. I landed multiple interviews, but each one hit the same wall. When employers asked about my separation and uncovered the details, progress halted. My record was a scarlet letter, full of punishments that painted me as an outcast, not the officer who had led flawless launch campaigns at Vandenberg. The rejections piled up, each one eroding my sense of worth, leaving me to question if I'd ever provide for my family again.

Housing turned into a catastrophe that shattered what little stability we had left. After separation, we were given until the end of 2023 to remain in privatized housing on Vandenberg Space Force Base while we transitioned. But in early November 2023, our life unraveled further when our house caught fire. I'll never forget my wife's phone call as I drove home with our oldest son. Her voice was eerily calm, masking shock, as she said, "Our house is on fire." I pulled up to our street, blocked by fire trucks and police cars, neighbors staring as firefighters battled the blaze. My wife and youngest children sat in the grass across the street, tears streaming down their faces. I approached in disbelief, my heart pounding, but relief flooded me when I saw everyone was unharmed. When my son and I bent down, we all hugged each other—my wife, my kids, and me—the crackle of the fire a grim reminder of our loss. We lost everything—either to the flames or smoke damage. Without renter's insurance, we were helpless, officially homeless, our belongings reduced to ash.

The privatized housing company paid to put us in a temporary lodging facility for a few weeks while we searched for a new home. We worked tirelessly with every resource we could find—agencies like the Red Cross stepped in to help—but the process was excruciating. We spent Thanksgiving 2023 in temporary lodging, with no job, no home, and nothing to our name but each other. It was the newest low point of my life, a moment where the mandate's ripple effect hit its cruelest peak: my separation, the fire, our homelessness—all cascading from a stand I took on principle. My wife's own PTSD, a burden she carried from her past, compounded our struggle, making every step feel heavier. We were literally torn to nothing, stripped of the life we'd built over 13 years, left with only the clothes on our backs and the love we held for each other.

My wife constantly reminded me we had each other, and she always tried to stay positive, even as the world around us crumbled. In a world that was crumbling, she was the one person who saw me at my lowest point and stood by my side to experience that lowest point with me. Her resilience strengthened mine, which together, got a family of eight through hell together, even if we didn't come out the other side completely whole. Her strength became our anchor, a quiet force that kept us going when everything else was gone. In December 2023, we secured a new rental home in Lompoc with the help of another agency for veterans—a modest place, but ours—and shortly after, I found a company willing to take a chance on me, a job that was a lifeline I couldn't refuse. That opportunity marked a turning point, and my gratitude for it remains profound, as it offered a path to rebuild after months of despair, a chance to provide for my family once more.

Those months forced me to confront a lesson I'd preached as a leader but never truly faced: seeking help isn't weakness—it's survival. I'd spent years priding myself on unbreakable resilience, leading teams through crises, but post-separation, I turned to local community resources to navigate our challenges. My transition taught me that true survival means protecting what matters most—my family—and fighting for them with every ounce of strength, even when it means letting go of pride.

Executive Order

On January 27, 2025, a spark of hope pierced the fog of my exile. President Donald Trump signed an executive order to reinstate all service members discharged for refusing the COVID-19 vaccine, with full back pay—a bold stroke to right the wrongs of a mandate that had gutted my career and fractured my family from 2021 to 2023. I stood in my living room and felt the weight of those lost years: the out-of-state home we'd bought and lost, the premature birth of my daughter Constance, the relentless strain that broke my marriage. If Trump was offering a path back, I owed it to my family to seize it. I wasn't just chasing a job—I was fighting for redemption.

The next week, I drove to Vandenberg Space Force Base, the place where my career had unraveled. I walked its corridors, a ghost in a familiar haunt, seeking answers from the legal office, defense counsel, personnel offices— anyone who could guide me through reinstatement. Their responses were a chorus of shrugs: no one knew who to contact or how to start. Undeterred, I called the Air Force's Total Force Service Center. "We have no guidance from the Department of Defense," they said, opening an "inquiry ticket" with a vague promise to follow up. I called weekly through February and March, each conversation a mirror of the last: "Still no guidance." Hope, once a flame, flickered in the bureaucracy's chill.

On April 8, 2025, the Air Force unveiled its reinstatement guidance, and I pored over it with a mix of anticipation and dread. What I found wasn't salvation—it was sabotage. The rules mocked Trump's intent: four-year service commitments, back pay slashed by civilian earnings, the guidance demanded others admit their separations were "freely chosen" without coercion. Applications were routed through the Board for Correction of Military Records, a creaking system unfit for thousands of cases. The promised "welcome back letters" from Secretary of Defense Pete Hegseth? A myth. My only contact was a curt email from the Service Center: "We have received a COVID-19 reinstatement website if you want to review," which linked to a page that offered more questions than answers. Someone, somewhere, had crafted this process not to heal but to hinder, indifferent to the lives left in the mandate's wreckage.

For two and a half months, I'd poured my energy into this fight—calls, visits, waiting—driven by the belief that justice was possible. But the guidance wasn't a bridge back; it was a wall. For my family, already scarred by the mandate's toll, I couldn't chase a hollow promise. I paused my pursuit, not out of defeat, but to wait for a process that truly honored the sacrifices of those cast aside. Thousands of us, stripped of our careers, stand together in this limbo, our trust in the system as shattered as our pasts. Trump's order was a beacon, but its light dims when those tasked to carry it falter. Leadership isn't in the signing of orders—it's in the fight to make them real.

Exile's Redemption

For two years, from 2021 to 2023, I lived in suffocating solitude, branded a criminal by the very institution I swore to serve. The DoD's COVID-19 vaccine mandate didn't just strip me of my career—it stripped me of my dignity, leaving me to feel like I was the only one enduring this nightmare. I was a Space Force officer, a father of six, a man who led flawless launch campaigns, yet I was reduced to an outcast, banned from government buildings at Vandenberg Space Force Base for 20 months. That exile, starting November 2, 2021, isolated me from my peers, my purpose, and my pride. I walked into my home office each day, powered on my computer, and faced the silence—not just the absence of voices, but the absence of belonging. The military I loved turned its back on me, and I felt like the only one in the world who dared to say no.

The ban wasn't about protecting anyone from COVID-19; I saw that then. It was about protecting the system from a "mind virus"—the dangerous idea that someone like me, standing against the mandate, might inspire others to question it too. Leadership feared the ripple effect of defiance, so they locked me out, ensuring my voice couldn't reach my peers. I led my team through the pandemic unvaccinated, keeping Vandenberg fully functional without a single COVID case, but suddenly I was a threat. Not to their health, but to their control. The isolation was a weapon, designed to make me feel like a criminal, a pariah whose moral stand was a crime against the chain of command. And it worked. I lay awake at night, the weight of that label pressing down, wondering if I was truly alone in this fight.

A few calls trickled in during those years—fellow service members, some from other branches, who battled the same mandate. They shared their stories of reprimands, separations, and shattered lives, their voices a faint echo of my own pain, and I spoke to a few members asking to share my story. But those conversations, though a flicker of connection, couldn't pierce the fog of isolation. They didn't ease the gnawing sense that I was a lone criminal, fighting a battle no one else could understand. My world shrank to my family, my routine, and the relentless psychological warfare of the Space Force's tactics—menial tasks, public shaming, and the ever-present threat of more punishment. I clung to my conviction, but the cost was a solitude so deep it felt like a second skin.

When I was involuntarily separated on August 31, 2023, after 13 years of service, the emotional wreckage overwhelmed me. I tried to detach completely, to bury the pain of those years and move forward as a civilian father in Lompoc, California. I focused on my children—coaching their sports, helping with homework, being the steady hand they needed—but the scars of that ordeal lingered, a silent ache I couldn't outrun. It wasn't until January 27, 2025, when President Trump signed an executive order to reinstate service members discharged for refusing the vaccine, that I felt a spark of hope. That spark ignited a fire when I created an account on X, seeking answers about reinstatement. What I found wasn't just information—it was a revelation.

On X, I discovered a vast, vibrant community of service members who were in the same boat as me, tens of thousands strong, actively fighting back against the mandate's injustice. They hailed from every branch—Army, Navy, Air Force, Marines, Space Force—resilient warriors who faced the same punishments, the same isolation, the same label of "criminal." Their posts were a battle cry: stories of defiance, legal battles, and a shared resolve to hold the military accountable. I scrolled through threads, my heart pounding, as I read accounts that mirrored my own—families torn apart, careers destroyed, yet a fierce determination to seek justice. This wasn't just a community; it was a force, some of our nation's most resilient and determined individuals, united by a betrayal we all endured. They weren't just surviving—they were fighting, and they had been doing so all along, even when I felt most alone.

I couldn't have been prouder to find that community or to join their fight—

a battle far from over. I was no longer a criminal but a brother-in-arms in a movement that refused to let the mandate's betrayal be the final word. We shared, and continue to share resources, legal strategies, and stories of hope, like Secretary of Defense Pete Hegseth's April 2025 declaration that the mandate was unlawful—a validation that fueled our fire. Together, we push for reinstatement, accountability, and restitution for ourselves and the tens of thousands of service members and families scarred by the mandate, and we continue to do these things, knowing the fight will stretch on for years. The isolation that had once defined my struggle dissolved in the strength of this collective stand. I had thought I was alone, but I had been part of a silent army—one now roaring and ready to rebuild what was broken.

Reflection Through the Fire

After discovering the X community in January 2025, I felt a weight lift—not the full burden of my exile, but enough to let me breathe again. For two years, I had carried the label of a criminal, an outcast in a military I'd served with pride for 13 years. The isolation had hollowed me out, leaving me to question not just my career, but my worth as a father and husband. My wife had seen me at my lowest—teleworking in silence, stripped of my uniform, unable to give our family the stability I'd promised—while I shielded our children from knowing the depth of my struggle. Finding tens of thousands of service members who shared my struggle was a lifeline, a reminder that I wasn't alone. But more than that, it forced me to look inward, to see the man I'd become through the fire of the mandate's betrayal.

That community didn't just validate my stand; it reshaped me. I began to see my fight through my children's eyes—not as a failure, but as a lesson in courage. I'd shielded them from the worst of it, deflecting their questions with half-truths to protect their innocence, but now I understood that my stand was part of their legacy too. One day, they'd ask why I refused the vaccine, why I let our family be torn apart. I'd tell them I stood firm because I valued integrity over compliance—a principle that holds steady, no matter the cost. That realization brought clarity. I wasn't just a father fighting to rebuild; I was a father fighting for a future where they'd never face the same betrayal I did.

This clarity also shifted my view of the military I'd loved. The Space Force had been my frontier, a place where I led teams to launch rockets and shape history. But the mandate exposed its flaws—leaders who valued orders over honor, systems that crushed rather than protected. I still believed in the military's mission, but I now saw its cracks with unflinching eyes. My fight wasn't just for me or my family anymore; it was for every service member who'd been cast aside, for a nation whose security depended on a force that had lost its way. Standing with that X community, I found a new purpose: to ensure the mandate's scars weren't in vain, to push for a military rebuilt on trust and accountability.

Unlawful

A single word can shift the ground beneath you. On April 23, 2025, that word was "unlawful," spoken by Secretary of Defense Pete Hegseth in a video that roared through the hearts of every service member scarred by the COVID-19 vaccine mandate. For me, a father of six whose family and career were torn apart from 2021 to 2023, it was a thunderclap of vindication, a long-awaited acknowledgment of the pain we'd endured. Two weeks later, on May 7, the Under Secretary of Defense cemented this truth in a memorandum, declaring the mandate a violation of justice. I stood in my kitchen, the news flickering on my phone, and felt the ghosts of those years—our lost home, my daughter Constance's fragile fight, our fractured marriage—stir with the promise of redemption. This wasn't just my moment; it was a reckoning for thousands whose lives the mandate had shattered.

The mandate was a sledgehammer, striking every service member, every family, in its path. For those of us who refused the vaccine, believing it wrong in our bones, we were branded criminals. We faced career-killing paperwork— LORs, tainted performance reports—punishments, lost promotions, isolation from peers, public shaming, and involuntary discharges that left us adrift in the civilian world. Others, staring down those same threats, chose voluntary separation, hoping to escape the shadow of punishment, only to carry regret like a stone. Some, with families to feed, took the vaccine against their instincts, their trust in leadership now a bitter aftertaste. Those who complied, misled on the vaccine's efficacy, grappled with broken faith in a system that promised protection. And then there were those who believed the promise of safety, only to face lifelong injuries from a vaccine they were told would shield them. No one escaped unscathed—not the refusers, not the coerced, not the misled, not the wounded. The mandate was a betrayal that rippled through bases, homes, and futures, leaving tens of thousands of us to pick up the pieces.

Secretary of Defense Pete Hegseth's declaration was a torch in the darkness. It validated every stand I'd taken, every sacrifice my family endured—Constance's premature birth, our savings drained, our unity fractured. It flung open doors to justice: legal recourse for those punished, VA benefits for those injured, and the promise of accountability for leaders who'd wielded the mandate like a weapon. Those commanders who'd shamed us, who'd prioritized compliance over compassion, now faced scrutiny for the lives they'd upended. This wasn't just a policy reversal; it was the first step toward restitution, a chance to heal the wounds of hundreds of thousands—service members, spouses, children—whose dreams were collateral damage in a war of orders.

Yet, as I watch Secretary of Defense Pete Hegseth's words loop on my screen, gratitude wrestles with grief. The truth is here, but it can't rebuild my career, restore my children's stolen stability, or erase the scars of those years. It's a victory, but a heavy one, tempered by the knowledge that justice moves slowly, and trust, once broken, mends even slower. For me, and for the thousands standing shoulder to shoulder in this moment, Hegseth's admission is a lifeline, but not an ending. We'll carry the fight forward—through courtrooms, VA clinics, and the quiet rebuilding of our lives—because when truth finally speaks, it demands more than acknowledgment. It demands action. And we, the betrayed, will push on, relentless, until justice is no longer a promise but a reality.

Impact on National Security

As an Air Force and Space Force captain with 13 years of service, whose career and family were upended by the COVID-19 vaccine mandate, I offer this chapter as my personal perspective, insight, and opinion on the national security crisis it unleashed—a crisis I've witnessed through my own experiences and the stories of countless others.

When Secretary of Defense Pete Hegseth declared the mandate "unlawful" on April 23, 2025, it marked a pivotal moment of vindication for those who resisted—a courageous step toward justice that shone a stark light on a national security threat brewing since 2021. Hegseth's declaration, backed by President Trump's administration, was a beacon of hope for the military community, acknowledging the deep wounds inflicted by the mandate and setting the stage to right those wrongs. From my perspective, the policy didn't merely disrupt individual lives; it fractured the foundation of the world's mightiest military, purging an estimated 50,000 troops who questioned an order they believed was wrong. These service members weren't just numbers— they were free thinkers, the kind willing to challenge hard decisions, ensuring missions succeed through critical thought, not blind obedience. Many had years of experience, their training valued in the millions per individual, a depth of expertise no new recruit can replicate. Their stories, shared through conversations and accounts I've read after the fact, reveal a loss that echoes across every branch, leaving a void our enemies can surely sense.

The mandate's impact on those who remained cuts even deeper, as I see it. The military today is a shadow of its former strength, divided between those who complied without question—unquestioning conformists who accepted the vaccine without hesitation—and those coerced into compliance, pressured by the need to secure a paycheck to maintain their way of life, to include caring for their families. Thousands of these service members now suffer vaccine injuries: heart problems, neurological disorders, cancer, diminished endurance—conditions that sap their ability to serve effectively. Beyond their physical toll, these injuries have shattered trust in the system they swore to defend. They were told the vaccine would protect them, that it would save lives, yet saw it fail to deliver and endured lies about its necessity—falsehoods that eroded their faith. The recent vindication under President Trump's administration and Hegseth's leadership, declaring the mandate unlawful, has finally brought these betrayals to light, exposing a system that failed its troops and deepening the fracture in morale that a fighting force needs to endure.

In my opinion, the most severe threat lies with the leaders who enforced this mandate—countless commanders who issued punishments that scarred lives across every rank and branch. Service members faced relentless persecution: reprimands, tainted performance reports, lost promotions, isolation, and involuntary discharges that left them adrift in the civilian world. These actions, now deemed unlawful, inflicted lifelong damage on troops and their families—shattered homes, stolen stability, careers reduced to nothing—while weakening mission readiness by depleting units of their most experienced members. Our adversaries have likely taken note of this vulnerability, a gaping wound in our national defense. Yet these commanders remain in positions of power, their accountability delayed, their presence a lingering threat to the integrity of the force.

These leaders must be held accountable, and I believe Hegseth, with his commitment to justice, can lead this charge—but it must be done in a carefully planned way, one that signifies justice is being served without publicly signaling a weak point in our military leadership. Failing to act risks further unlawful actions, endangering the new recruits who now step into this fractured force. The trust of our troops, the readiness of our units, and the safety of our nation hang in the balance. In my view, as someone who lived through the mandate's fallout, this mandate has done more harm to our national security than all our enemies combined—a crisis our adversaries are undoubtedly aware of, watching for any chance to exploit our weakened state.

Restitution and accountability for the damage caused by the COVID-19 mandate cannot be ignored—it's a matter of survival for our military and our nation. I believe the Secretary of Defense, building on the good he's already done for our community, must act swiftly, establishing a special unit to address this crisis, composed of unbiased individuals and some of the highly qualified service members who were purged. This unit could operate behind closed doors, rectifying the damage discreetly to safeguard our national security interests while ensuring justice is served. Commanders who broke the law must be removed, their replacements carefully vetted to ensure they're neither unquestioning conformists nor too disillusioned to lead with integrity. The stakes are nothing less than the soul of our military—a force that must be rebuilt with trust, strength, and honor at its core. These are my insights, shaped by my journey and the collective pain of so many others; I urge readers to consider this crisis through their own lens, recognizing the urgent need to act before it's too late.

Nuremberg Comparison

The Nuremberg Trials of 1945–1946, which prosecuted Nazi leaders for war crimes, established a principle that resonates with the collective resistance of tens of thousands of U.S. service members to the Department of Defense's COVID-19 vaccine mandate in 2021: individuals must refuse unlawful orders, even at great personal cost. At Nuremberg, figures like Hermann Göring and Rudolf Hess claimed they were "just following orders," but the trials rejected this defense, holding them accountable for atrocities like the Holocaust. This precedent of moral responsibility over blind obedience mirrors the stand taken by countless service members against the DoD's mandate—a directive later declared unlawful by Secretary of Defense Pete Hegseth in 2025.

Though the Pfizer-BioNTech vaccine received full FDA approval under the name "Comirnaty" on August 23, 2021, that version was never made available to service members. Instead, doses remained under Emergency Use Authorization, making the mandate legally questionable from the start. At the time, many of us relied on our moral guidance, experiences working through the COVID pandemic, and gut feelings to refuse the vaccine, lacking the legal understanding or access to challenge the narrative we were given until later. Across the military, tens of thousands resisted, facing involuntary separations, career losses, and personal hardships, despite the mandate's eventual rescission in 2023.

At Nuremberg, the rejection of the "superior orders" defense emphasized individual accountability. Defendants were held responsible for following directives that enabled systemic abuses, costing millions of lives. While the context differs vastly, the principle remains: one must resist orders that contravene moral or legal standards. The collective defiance of service members against the DoD's mandate reflects this Nuremberg legacy—a legacy of standing firm against directives that overstep ethical boundaries.

This connection gained clarity in 2025, when Secretary of Defense Pete Hegseth declared the vaccine mandate issued by the previous administration unlawful. Hegseth's statement mirrored the Nuremberg Trials' focus on accountability for those who issue and enforce unlawful orders. Just as the trials sought justice for systemic abuses by prosecuting Nazi leaders, Hegseth's declaration underscored the need for transparency and redress for the service members impacted by the mandate. It validated the resistance of tens of thousands, affirming that their refusal to comply was grounded in a broader ethical framework.

The Nuremberg Trials highlighted the dangers of blind obedience, a lesson that echoes through the experiences of those affected by the mandate. The DoD's directive, now officially deemed unlawful, relied on compliance, often disregarding the toll on service members. Thousands faced coercion and career-ending consequences, their lives upended by a policy that violated their rights. Nuremberg exposed the catastrophic outcomes of following unlawful orders; the mandate's fallout reveals the modern-day costs of systemic overreach in the military. Hegseth's 2025 statement brought this parallel into focus, emphasizing that resisting unlawful orders remains a moral imperative.

The fight for accountability and restitution for those harmed by the mandate echoes the Nuremberg Trials' pursuit of justice. The trials set a precedent for future generations, ensuring systemic abuses are met with transparency and redress. Similarly, the call for justice persists for the tens of thousands of service members and their families who suffered under the mandate's enforcement. Hegseth's acknowledgment strengthens this demand, aligning their collective struggle with a historical standard of moral responsibility— a standard that demands questioning authority when it oversteps ethical bounds.

The Nuremberg Trials remain a reminder that history judges not by obedience, but by integrity. The stand taken by countless service members against the DoD's mandate reflects this principle: unlawful orders must be defied, even at great cost. Secretary Hegseth's 2025 declaration reinforces this lesson, affirming that their resistance was a necessary stand for justice in our era. The legacy of Nuremberg calls for continued accountability, ensuring that the sacrifices of those impacted guide us toward a more just future.

A Path Forward

The DoD's COVID-19 vaccine mandate left lasting damage on our military and its families, a crisis I've lived through as an Air Force and Space Force officer with 13 years of service. The current system to address such injustices, specifically the Board for Correction of Military Records (BCMR) process, is broken and must be abandoned entirely—it's not designed to handle a crisis of this magnitude in a timely manner, as its case-by-case approach has already proven ineffective. We've seen packages returned without proper review, and service members denied the relief they desperately sought, leaving tens of thousands of claims bottlenecked and delaying justice for years. I offer my perspective on how we can heal these wounds, drawing on the momentum from Secretary of Defense Pete Hegseth's declaration on April 23, 2025, that the mandate was unlawful. This chapter reflects my personal opinions and insights, shaped by my journey, and is not intended to assert legal or factual claims against the DoD or its entities. I recognize there are many ways to address this crisis, and the solutions I propose here are my personal starting point—a foundation of the basic steps I believe must happen to make things right. I propose detailed procedures, authorization structures, and a training scenario to ensure this crisis informs future military leadership, rebuilding a force rooted in trust, readiness, and honor.

Task Force Setup

I believe the DoD should establish a dedicated task force to address the mandate's fallout, operating under the authority of the Under Secretary of Defense for Personnel and Readiness (USD P&R), who oversees personnel policy and readiness. The USD P&R, reporting to Secretary Hegseth, would initiate the task force via a formal memorandum, outlining its mission to focus on restitution, accountability, and reform. Given the scale of the crisis—tens of thousands of affected service members—I propose a robust team of 200–300 members, including DoD civilians, medical experts, and reinstated service members who were purged, selected by a panel convened by the Assistant Secretary of Defense for Manpower and Reserve Affairs. This larger group, divided into regional subcommittees, would ensure timely processing of cases, with each subcommittee handling claims from specific service branches or geographic areas. The task force would operate discreetly, holding closed-door meetings at the Pentagon or secure virtual sessions, to avoid signaling weakness to adversaries while coordinating with service branches via encrypted channels.

Restitution

For restitution, I propose the task force develop a program, authorized by the USD P&R under existing legal authority to correct military records, to process claims for financial compensation, covering full back pay in accordance with President Trump's executive order intentions, lost wages, all medical bills incurred by the family after separation due to lost medical coverage, medical expenses for vaccine-related injuries, and counseling or therapy for any family member who needs it to address years of instability. To address the BCMR's shortcomings, I suggest a temporary "Mandate Restitution Board" (MRB), established by the USD P&R, with streamlined procedures to batch-process claims, allowing for mass reinstatement of purged service members with restored ranks, benefits, and expunged mandate-related reprimands. Decisions would be appealable to the Secretary of each branch (e.g., Secretary of the Air Force). Funding would come from the DoD's Operations and Maintenance budget, reallocated by the Under Secretary of Defense (Comptroller) through established financial management regulations, ensuring no new congressional appropriation is needed initially. This process would bring experienced troops back into the fold, strengthening readiness without compromising security.

Accountability

Accountability, as I see it, requires the task force to conduct a "Leadership Accountability Review" (LAR), authorized by the Secretary of Defense under existing regulations governing military personnel actions. The LAR would investigate commanders who issued punitive measures during the mandate, using existing records like LORs, UCMJ punishments, and OPRs, accessible via personal files. The task force would establish a review board, chaired by a retired flag officer appointed by the USD P&R, to assess each case, focusing on actions deemed unjust, such as unwarranted career sabotage. Commanders found culpable would face removal via administrative separation proceedings, initiated by their branch's personnel command (e.g., Air Force Personnel Center for USAF officers). Replacements would be vetted by a selection board convened by the Assistant Secretary of Defense for Force Management Policy, prioritizing leaders who demonstrate ethical decision-making and support for critical thinking, ensuring they rebuild trust within units. For retired commanders who were negligent in their actions or caused severe harm to the well-being of service members, their families, and national security, the review board would recommend their recall to service to ensure they are held accountable through formal proceedings.

Medical Care

To address health concerns, I suggest the task force oversee a "Vaccine Injury Support Program" (VISP), authorized by the Assistant Secretary of Defense for Health Affairs under regulations governing military health services. The

VISP would provide specialized care at military treatment facilities like Walter Reed, covering conditions like heart or neurological issues, with long-term monitoring via the Defense Health Agency's electronic health records system. The program would also meticulously track and document every vaccine-related injury reported by service members and veterans, creating a comprehensive database to fully understand and quantify the extent of the harm caused by the mandate. Mental health support would be integrated through the Military Health System for active members, offering counseling at base-level clinics, coordinated by the Defense Health Agency's Behavioral Health Branch.

I also propose a "Family Stabilization Fund" (FSF), funded through the DoD's Morale, Welfare, and Recreation budget, authorized by the USD P&R under existing welfare regulations. The FSF would cover relocation costs, housing support, or therapy, managed by base-level Family Support Centers, ensuring families aren't left to rebuild alone.

VA Care

For veterans no longer in service, I propose integrating VA care, authorized by the Under Secretary for Health at the Department of Veterans Affairs under existing legal authority, providing access to VA medical centers for specialized treatment of vaccine-related injuries. Additionally, the VA should establish a specific disability rating category for COVID-19 vaccine injuries, processed through the Veterans Benefits Administration, ensuring fair compensation and care for conditions like myocarditis or neurological disorders, with ratings determined via the VA Schedule for Rating Disabilities (VASRD). Mental health support would be integrated through the VA for veterans, offering counseling at VA facilities, coordinated by the VA's Mental Health Services.

Reforms

Reforming policy, in my opinion, starts with the task force drafting a "Medical Mandate Policy Directive" (MMPD), issued by the USD P&R under its authority over personnel policy. The MMPD would mandate robust informed consent processes, requiring service members to receive detailed briefings on medical interventions, documented via signed consent forms stored in their personnel files. Independent oversight would come from a new Medical Ethics Oversight Board, established by the Assistant Secretary of Defense for Health Affairs, to review future mandates for safety and necessity. Exemptions respecting individual beliefs would be processed through a standardized form, reviewed by a chaplain-led board at each major command, ensuring no penalties for denial, per my vision of a fair system. I believe leadership training should be updated via the Defense Equal Opportunity Management Institute, incorporating ethical decision-making modules into existing courses, fostering a culture where questioning orders is valued, preserving the critical thinking our military needs.

Training for Future Service Members

I envision this crisis becoming a case study in military training programs— BMT, OTS, ROTC, service academies, Squadron Officer School, and leadership courses like the Air War College. The "Mandate Crisis Scenario" would be integrated into curricula by the respective training commands (e.g., Air Education and Training Command for USAF programs), authorized by the Chief of Staff of each service branch under existing legal authority for the Air Force, as an example. The scenario would present a hypothetical mandate, detailing its impact on troops and families, and task trainees with developing ethical responses, balancing mission needs with troop welfare. At BMT, recruits would role-play as junior enlisted facing pressure to comply, debating their options in small groups. At OTS and ROTC, officer candidates would analyze the scenario through leadership lenses, proposing policy reforms in written essays. Academies would incorporate it into military history courses, while Squadron Officer School and leadership training would use it in war-gaming exercises, simulating task force operations to address fallout. This training, in my view, would ensure future leaders learn from our pain, embedding ethical decision-making into the military's core.

Restoring Trust

On April 23, 2025, Secretary Hegseth took a significant first step by publicly acknowledging the unlawfulness of the COVID-19 vaccine mandate, describing it as "unfair, overbroad, and unnecessary." He issued a memorandum directing the Under Secretary of Defense for Personnel and Readiness to facilitate the reinstatement of affected service members, including the removal of adverse actions like less-than-fully-honorable discharges, and offered an apology for the mandate's implementation. To build on this initial action, I believe Secretary Hegseth should provide regular updates for the remainder of his time in this position, demonstrating positive steps in the right direction to rebuild trust and readiness. This could pair with a recruitment campaign, managed by the Defense Human Resources Activity, offering incentives like signing bonuses or accelerated career tracks to bring back experienced veterans. As an officer who lived through this crisis, I believe these steps can rebuild a military where honor and trust fuel our readiness to face any threat.

Echoes of Betrayal

My story is a single voice in a chorus of tens of thousands, each resounding with the pain of service members and families crushed by the DoD's COVID-19 vaccine mandate—a policy that turned the world's greatest fighting force against its own. From 2021 to 2023, I stood firm against an order I believed was unlawful, watching it tear my family apart: our home lost, my daughter Constance born fighting for breath, our marriage stretched to the breaking point. But I was not alone. The mandate unleashed a psychological war, wielding fear, shame, and punishment to coerce compliance with a vaccine that caused more harm than the virus it claimed to defeat. It branded refusers like me as criminals, stripped us of careers, and left us adrift. It coerced others into compliance, only to betray them with lifelong injuries or shattered trust in a system that promised protection. Families fractured, dreams dissolved, and the military's soul bore scars no medal can hide.

The cost was catastrophic—not just to us, but to the nation we swore to defend. The mandate drove out tens of thousands of elite troops, warriors whose expertise no recruitment drive can replace. It injured thousands more, their bodies and futures marred by a vaccine sold as salvation. Worst of all, it left a force led by officers who, in their zeal for compliance, shattered lives with a ruthlessness most can't fathom. This wasn't just a policy failure; it was a betrayal of trust that weakened force readiness and imperiled national security, eroding the very foundation of the world's mightiest military. The DoD's gravest mistake wasn't the mandate itself—it was believing it could break us without consequence.

Healing this wound demands action, not promises. It will take years of relentless work, a coalition of courageous leaders, and a commitment to truth to rebuild what was lost. Thousands of us—battle-tested, mandate-scarred troops—stand ready to answer the call. We're not just survivors; we're builders, eager to restore our military's strength and ensure no service member faces such betrayal again. I call on the President and Secretary of Defense Pete Hegseth to harness this force, to turn our resolve into a cornerstone of renewal for the greater good of our nation. The clock is ticking, and the stakes are nothing less than the soul of our military.

This book is my plea to those who lead, or will one day lead. If you hold power, or aspire to, let these pages be your guide. Every person you encounter—every soldier, spouse, child—carries a universe of dreams, struggles, and triumphs. Know them. Respect them. Lead them with the dignity they deserve, whether you command or follow, because leadership flows both ways. Your choices shape not just outcomes, but lives—families, futures, nations. Create an environment where trust thrives, and it will reflect back tenfold. Betray it, and the cost will echo for generations. I've seen both sides of that truth, and I carry its weight every day.

To you, the reader, who've walked these pages with us, thank you for bearing witness to our story. Your compassion fuels the fight ahead. Don't let this end here—share these lessons, demand better, lead better. For the thousands still scarred by the mandate, for the military we cherish, this is not a conclusion but a call. Together, we'll fight to restore our military and hold leaders accountable, ensuring this betrayal never happens again.

Epilogue

Looking back on my 13 years of service, I see a journey marked by duty, sacrifice, and an unyielding commitment to my principles. The COVID-19 vaccine mandate tested me in ways I never imagined—pushing me to defy an unlawful order, separate from the Space Force I helped build, and rebuild a life for my family amidst uncertainty. The scars of that crisis remain, etched in the financial struggles, the sleepless nights worrying over my youngest's health, and the lingering distrust toward a system I once swore to serve. But those scars also tell a story of resilience, of a father who fought for his children, and of a man who learned that leadership isn't about blind obedience—it's about doing what's right, even when it's the harder path.

Writing this memoir has been a way to process the pain, to honor the service members and families who endured the mandate's fallout, and to offer a path forward for a military I still believe in. My children have been my anchor through it all, their laughter and trust reminding me why I kept going. My wife's unwavering support gave me the strength to face each day, even when the odds felt insurmountable. Although we emerged from this as a broken family, we somehow found ourselves stronger, grounded in faith and a renewed sense of purpose.

Through those 13 years in the Air Force and Space Force, I learned that priorities change. The young boy I once was, who dreamed of growing up to be a pilot and astronaut, had to adjust those dreams when life demanded more. I chose to prioritize my family instead, ensuring they could grow up free to chase their own childhood dreams—whether that's reaching for the stars or carving their own path on solid ground. If I could go back and do it over again, I wouldn't change a thing, because every choice led me to them, and to the man I am now.

Throughout my experience battling the COVID-19 vaccine mandate—and the fallout that came with standing up against it—one thing became painfully clear: systems fail when they forget the humanity of the people inside them. Whether it's the military, a school, a corporation, or a family, once we start treating people like numbers, compliance tools, or problems to manage, we've already lost something we may not get back. Every policy, every order, every decision touches someone's real life. When we prioritize efficiency, appearance, or control over people, we damage more than just morale—we damage trust, relationships, and lives.

In the end, none of the recognition we earn—whether it's medals, promotions, or career achievements—follows us beyond this life. Those things may represent success in the moment, but they don't carry forward. What does endure is the impact we have on others. The way we treat people—especially when no one is watching—can leave a lasting imprint that extends far beyond the individual. Every interaction has the potential to shape someone's path, influence their choices, or affect how they show up for others. That's why it matters. Treat people like they matter—because you don't know what kind of impact your actions may have, not only on them, but on everyone they're connected to.

At night, after dinner is cleaned up, the day's activities are done, and teeth are brushed, I tuck each of my kids into bed, then lie alone in my room, still hearing the silence—the kind that lingers after something has been broken. It still carries the weight of all we've lost—my career, our family, our stability—but now it also holds a hard-won lesson. You have to find what keeps you going through the darkest of times and hold on to it with all that you've got. I've learned to embrace the silent nights, letting them guide my reflections on moments that reveal a stark truth: we have no control over the things that happen to us in life, so adjust your mindset as needed, and learn to enjoy the ride.

Glossary

B-52 Bomber: A long-range, subsonic, jet-powered strategic bomber operated by the U.S. Air Force, known for its versatility and ability to carry nuclear and conventional weapons, in service since the 1950s.

Chain of Command: A hierarchical structure in the military dictating the flow of authority and orders from superiors to subordinates.

Delta Commander (previously Wing Commander): A senior military officer responsible for leading a delta (formerly a wing), a larger organizational unit overseeing multiple squadrons, managing operations and strategic objectives.

Falcon 9: A reusable rocket developed by SpaceX, used for launching satellites and crew to orbit.

Fleet Surveillance: The process of monitoring and ensuring the success of non-government-owned space missions, such as commercial launches, through oversight, risk management, and technical analysis, akin to mission assurance for government missions.

Flight Commander: A military officer responsible for leading a flight, a small unit within a squadron.

Involuntary Separation: The forced discharge of a service member from the military, often due to disciplinary actions.

Mandate Rescission: The official cancellation of the COVID-19 vaccine mandate by the Department of Defense in 2023, ending the requirement for service members to be vaccinated.

Minotaur Rockets (Converted for Small Payloads): A family of U.S. rockets, repurposed from decommissioned intercontinental ballistic missiles, used to launch small payloads into orbit, often for military and government missions.

Mission Assurance: The process of ensuring a space mission's success through oversight, risk management, and technical analysis.

NASA Ascent Abort-2 Mission: A 2019 NASA test mission that demonstrated the Orion spacecraft's Launch Abort System, ensuring crew safety by simulating an emergency abort during ascent, conducted at Cape Canaveral.

National Security Space Launch: A program ensuring the U.S. military's access to space for national security purposes, involving launches of military payloads.

Psychological Warfare: Tactics used to intimidate or demoralize, such as isolation and public shaming, often employed during mandate enforcement.

RC-135 Reconnaissance Aircraft: A family of U.S. Air Force aircraft, including the RC-135 Rivet Joint, used for intelligence, surveillance, and reconnaissance missions, equipped with advanced sensors to collect electronic and signals intelligence.

Remote Launch Operations: Conducting space launches using remote systems to monitor and control operations from a distance.

Space Launch Complex: A designated area on a military base equipped for rocket launches.

Spacelift Operations: The process of launching payloads into space, encompassing preparation, launch, and recovery.

Squadron Commander: A military officer responsible for leading a squadron, a unit typically composed of several flights, overseeing operations and personnel.

Vaccine Mandate: A Department of Defense policy from 2021 requiring all service members to receive the COVID-19 vaccine, later declared unlawful in 2025.

Voluntary Separation: A service member's request to leave the military voluntarily.

Western Range: A region managed by Vandenberg Space Force Base for space launches, ensuring national space access.

X-37B Space Plane: An unmanned, reusable spacecraft operated by the U.S. Space Force, designed for long-duration orbital missions to test advanced space technologies, capable of autonomous reentry and landing.

About the Author

Joshua Zermeno, born on July 4, 1987, and raised in Southern California, is a former U.S. Air Force and Space Force officer. After graduating from Arizona State University with a mechanical engineering degree and a private pilot's license, he joined the Air Force and began his career as a mechanic on the B-52 bomber. As an Airman First Class, he was selected for both Officer Training School and Undergraduate Pilot Training. Graduating second in his class, he went on to work RC-135 reconnaissance aircraft missions, then shifted career paths once again, moving from flight crew to space launch operations at Vandenberg Space Force Base. There, his team of 37 executed nine flawless campaigns, sending 304 satellites and two astronauts into orbit; he contributed to NASA's Ascent Abort-2 mission, oversaw Minotaur vehicle transport across four U.S. sites, managed X-37B Orbital Test Vehicle integration, maintained seven key launch facilities, and drove Western Range strategies for national space access, before being selected to commission in the United States Space Force. In 2021, he fulfilled a moral obligation to disobey an unlawful order by resisting the DoD's COVID-19 vaccine mandate, leading to his involuntary separation despite the mandate's eventual rescission. His memoir, Disobeying An Unlawful Order, recounts this fight for freedom. Now, Zermeno seeks accountability for those who harmed tens of thousands of service members and their families, and restitution for those impacted.